MW00813588

REXTOOTH STUDIOS

HOWL
A NEW LOOK AT
THE BIG BAD WOLF

WRITTEN & ILLUSTRATED BY TED RECHLIN

EDITOR ANNE RECHLIN

COPYRIGHT © 2019 BY TED RECHLIN

PUBLISHED BY REXTOOTH STUDIOS, BOZEMAN, MONTANA

PRODUCED BY SWEETGRASS BOOKS, HELENA, MONTANA

ISBN: 978-1-59152-246-1

COVER DESIGN BY TED RECHLIN

 PRINTED IN THE UNITED STATES OF AMERICA

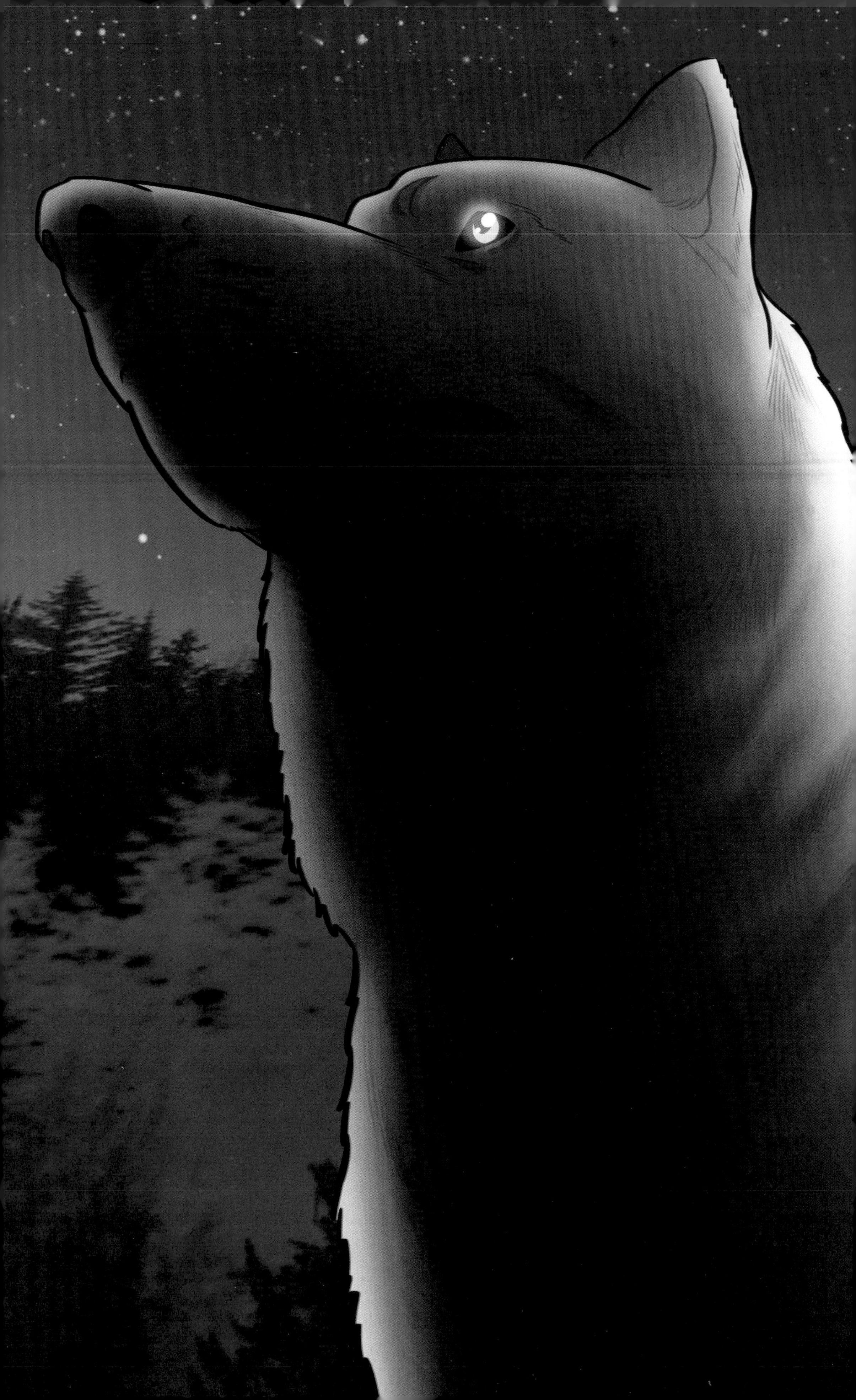

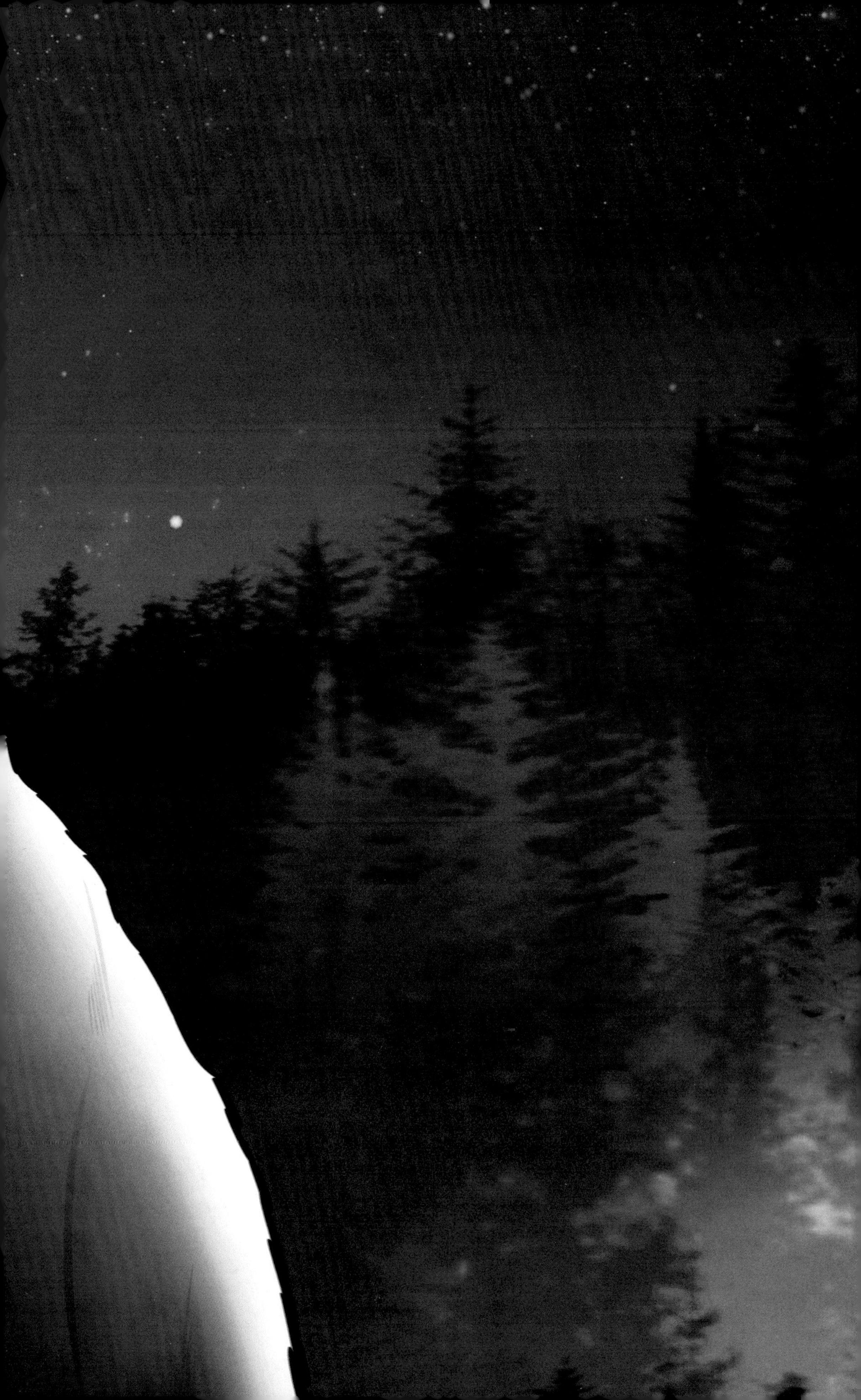

LOBO

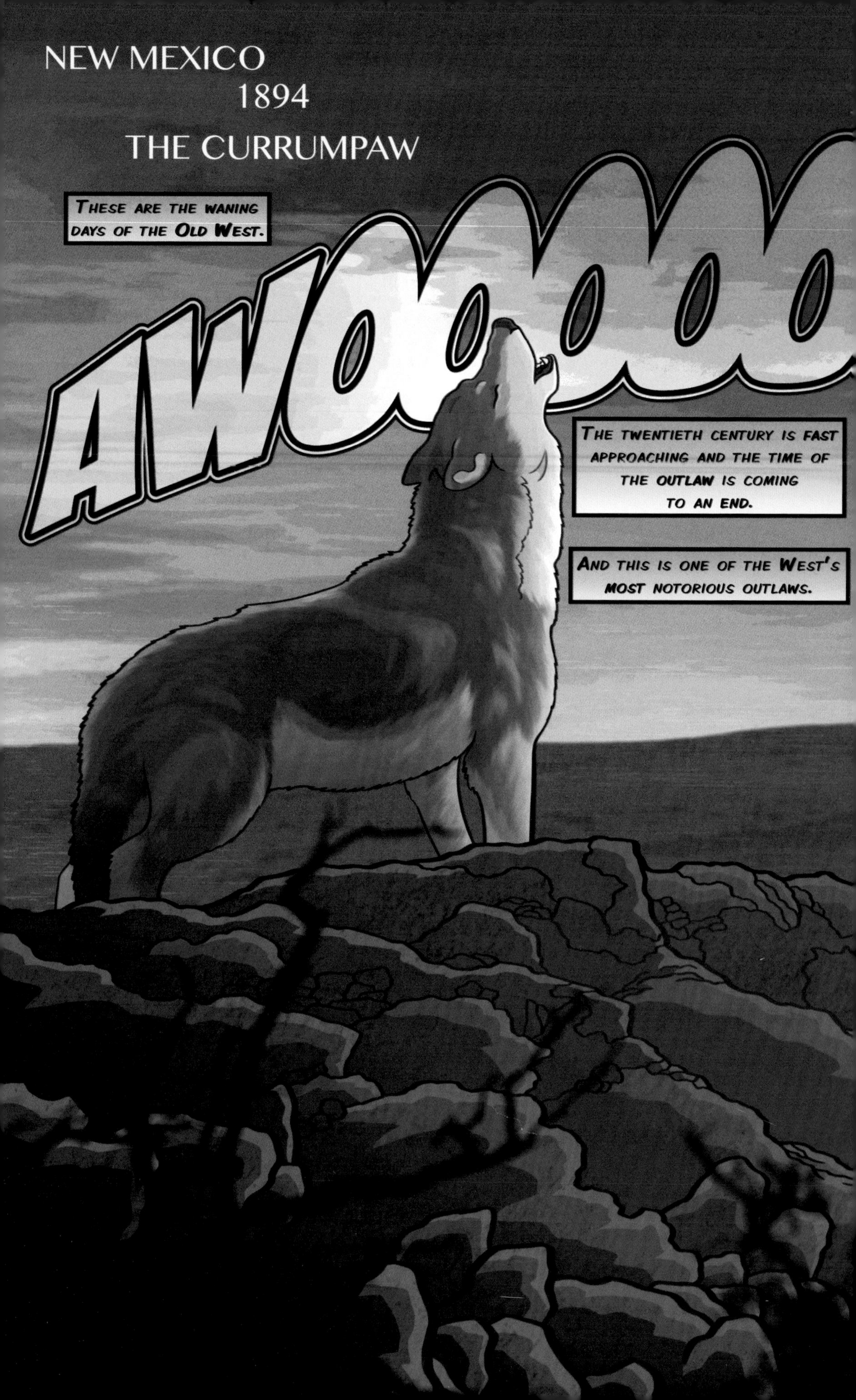
NEW MEXICO
1894
THE CURRUMPAW
THESE ARE THE WANING DAYS OF THE OLD WEST.
AWOOOOOO
THE TWENTIETH CENTURY IS FAST APPROACHING AND THE TIME OF THE OUTLAW IS COMING TO AN END.
AND THIS IS ONE OF THE WEST'S MOST NOTORIOUS OUTLAWS.

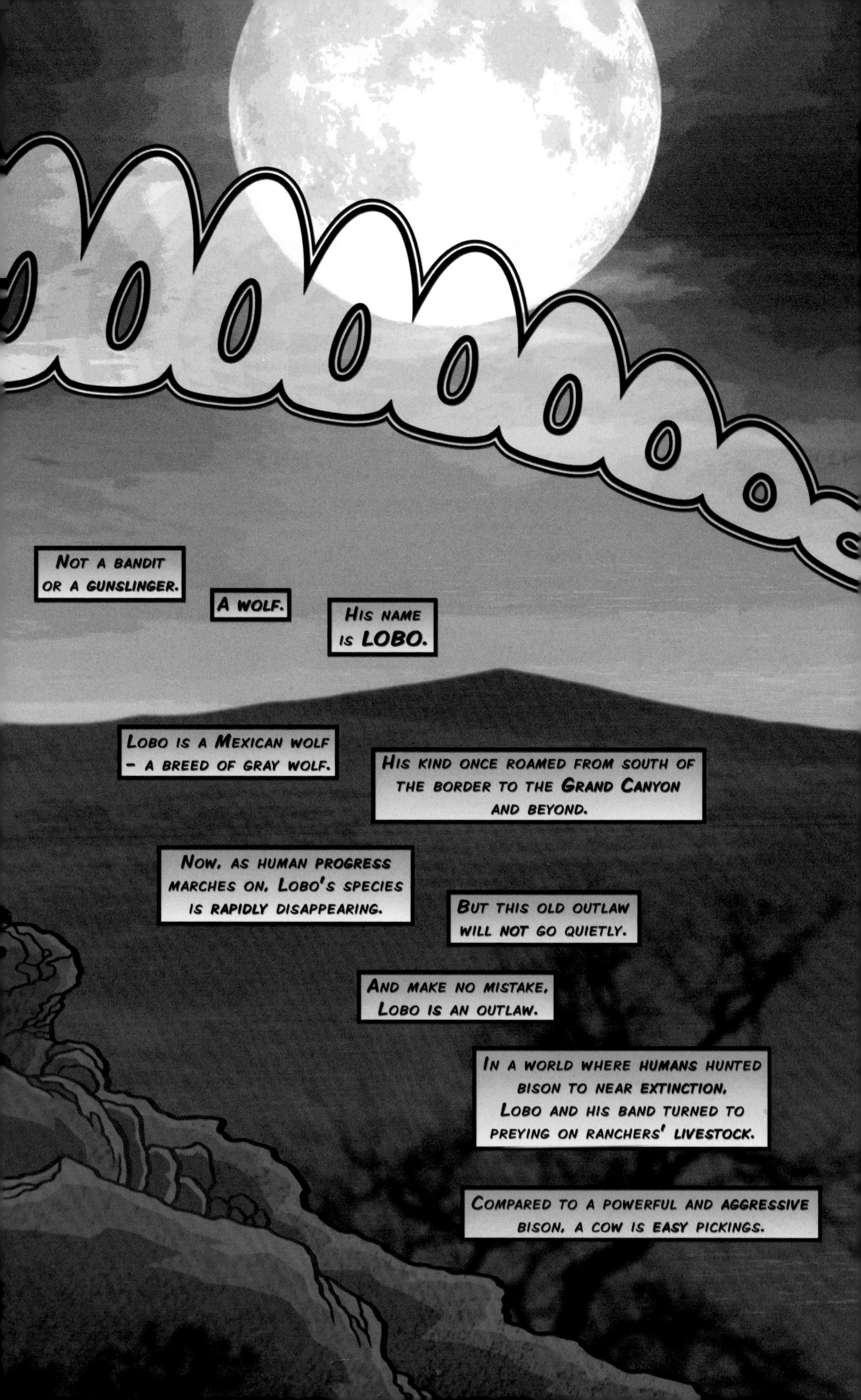
Not a bandit or a gunslinger.
A wolf.
His name is LOBO.
Lobo is a Mexican wolf – a breed of gray wolf.
His kind once roamed from south of the border to the Grand Canyon and beyond.
Now, as human progress marches on, Lobo's species is rapidly disappearing.
But this old outlaw will not go quietly.
And make no mistake, Lobo is an outlaw.
In a world where humans hunted bison to near extinction, Lobo and his band turned to preying on ranchers' livestock.
Compared to a powerful and aggressive bison, a cow is easy pickings.

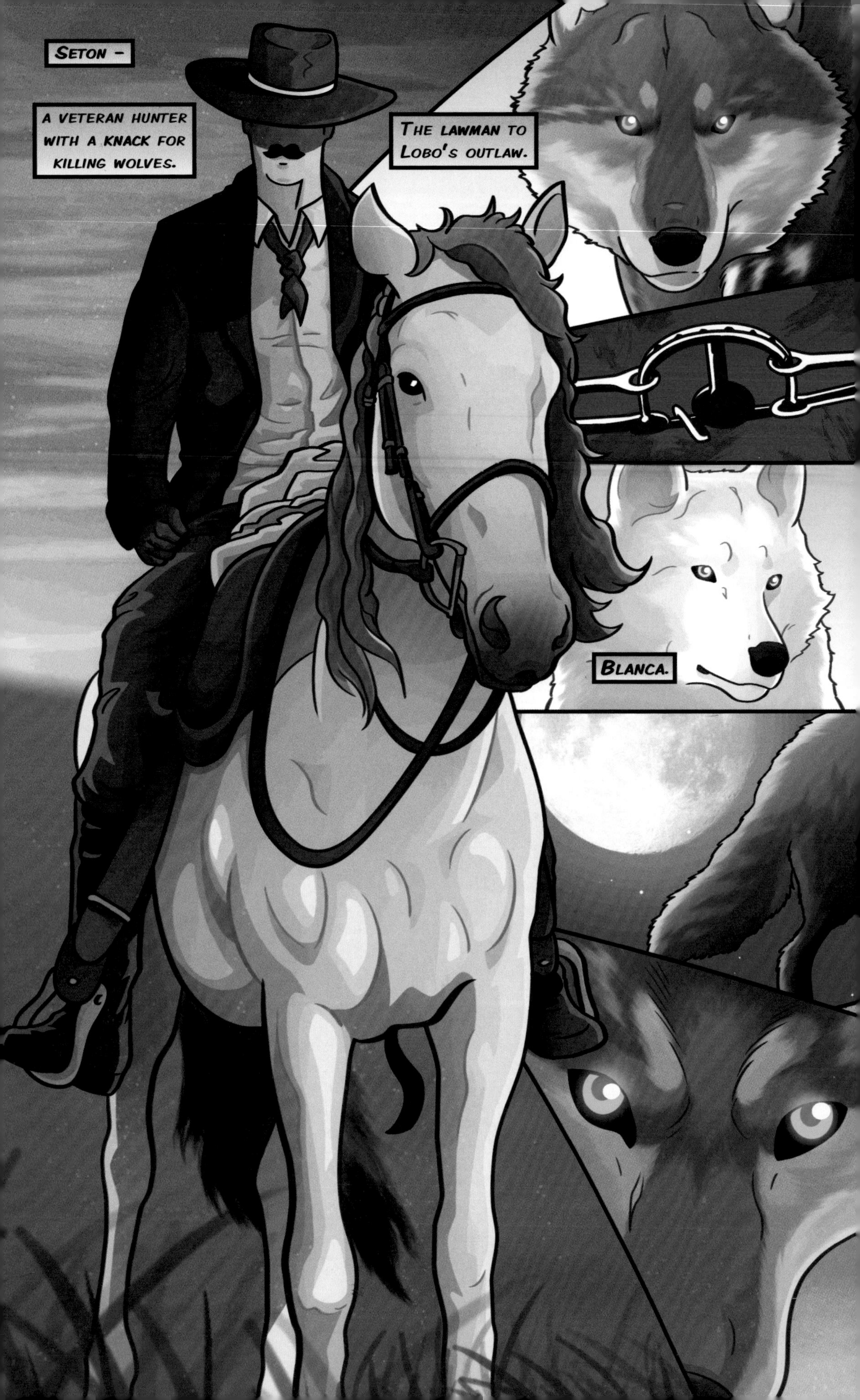
SETON -
A VETERAN HUNTER WITH A KNACK FOR KILLING WOLVES.
THE LAWMAN TO LOBO'S OUTLAW.
BLANCA.

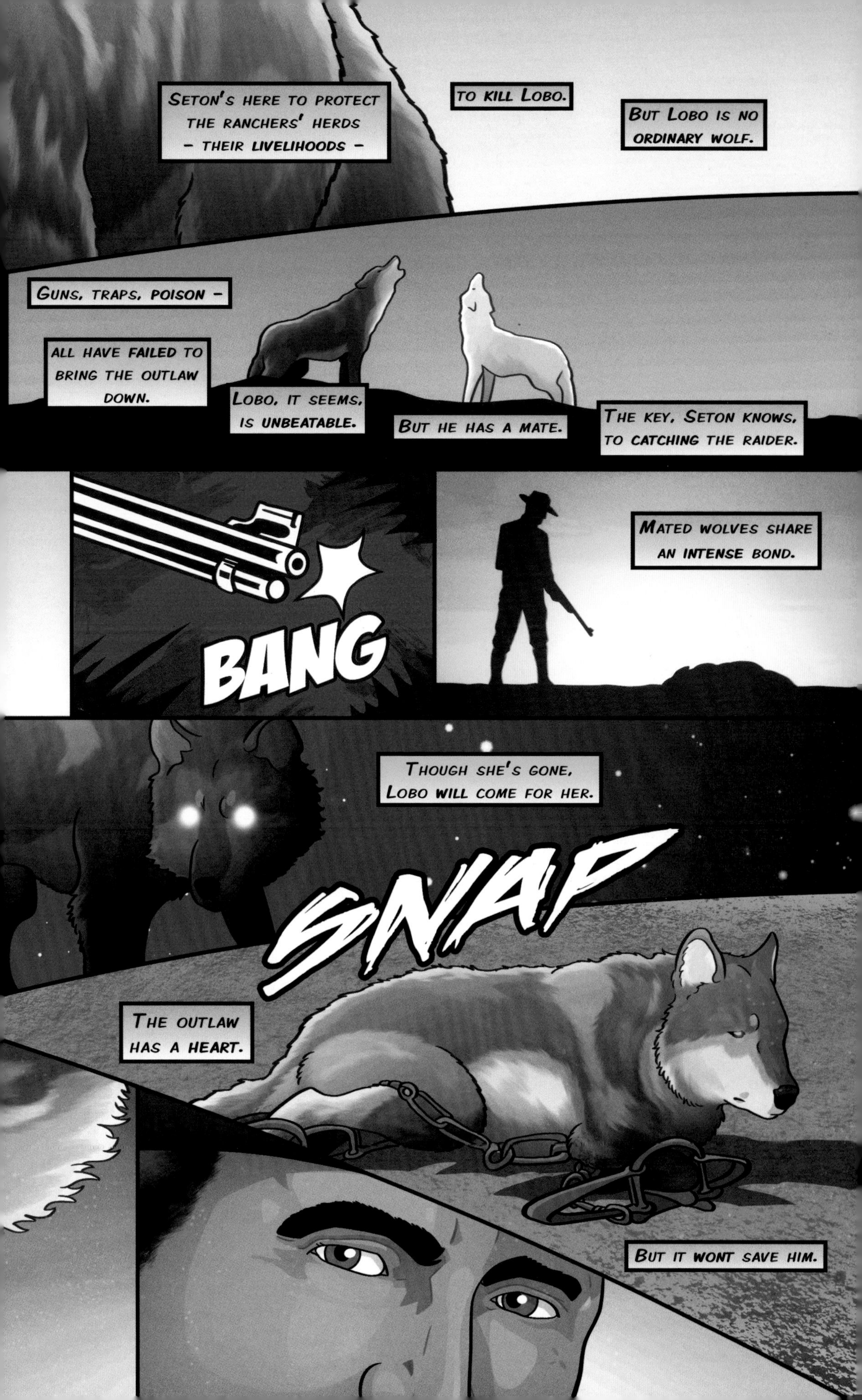
Seton's here to protect the ranchers' herds - their livelihoods -
to kill Lobo.
But Lobo is no ordinary wolf.
Guns, traps, poison -
all have failed to bring the outlaw down.
Lobo, it seems, is unbeatable.
But he has a mate.
The key, Seton knows, to catching the raider.
BANG
Mated wolves share an intense bond.
Though she's gone, Lobo will come for her.
SNAP
The outlaw has a heart.
But it wont save him.

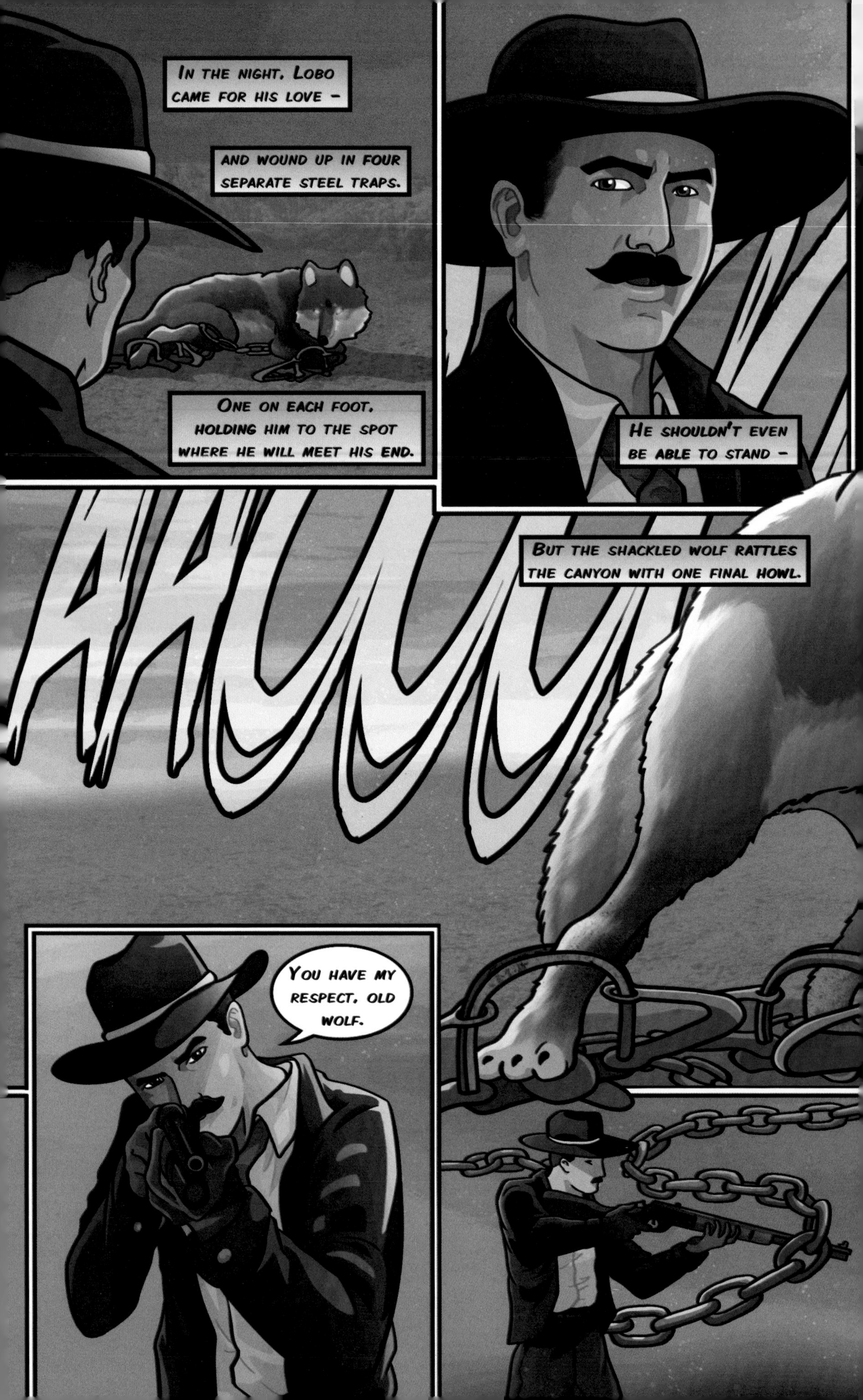

In the night, Lobo came for his love -
and wound up in four separate steel traps.
One on each foot, holding him to the spot where he will meet his end.
He shouldn't even be able to stand -
AHUUU
But the shackled wolf rattles the canyon with one final howl.
You have my respect, old wolf.

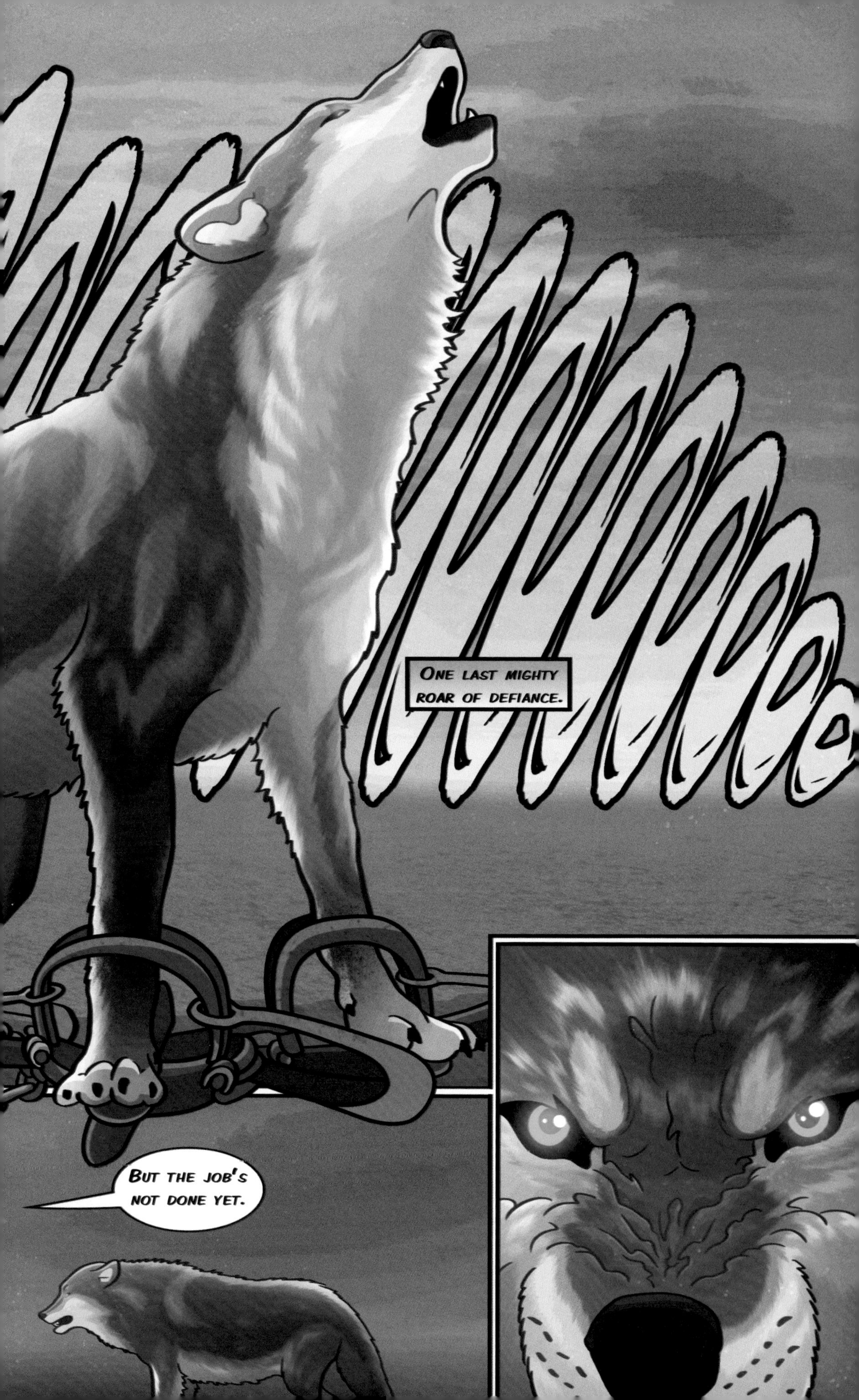
One last mighty roar of defiance.
But the job's not done yet.

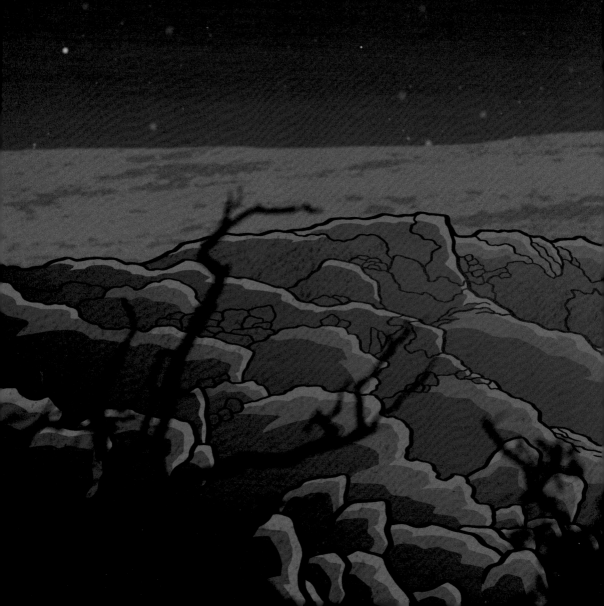

NEW MEXICO

1976

NEARLY ONE HUNDRED YEARS SINCE LOBO, AND DECADES SINCE THE LAST WOLF WAS SHOT DEAD —

THE HILLS AND CANYONS ARE SILENT.

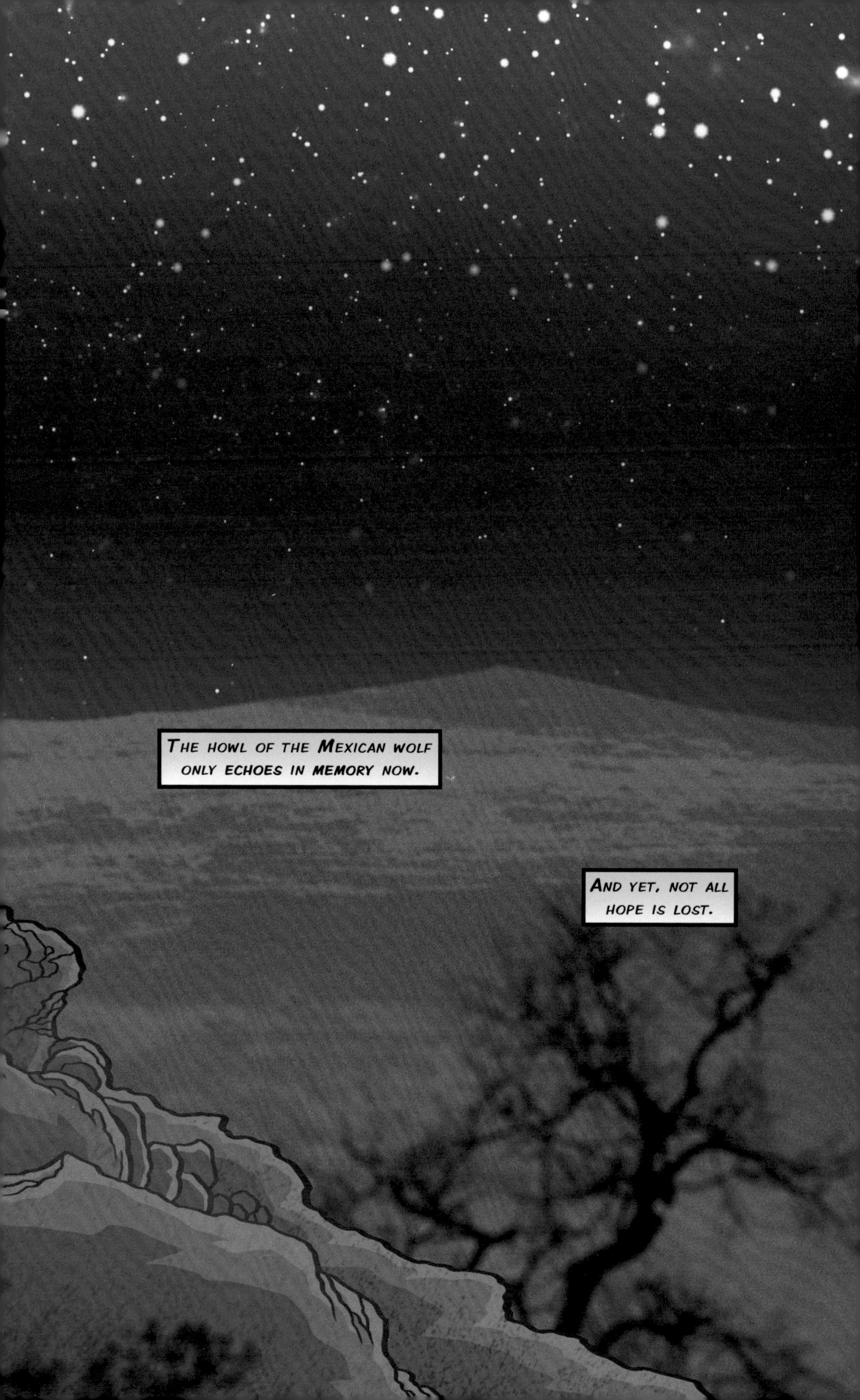
THE HOWL OF THE MEXICAN WOLF ONLY ECHOES IN MEMORY NOW.
AND YET, NOT ALL HOPE IS LOST.

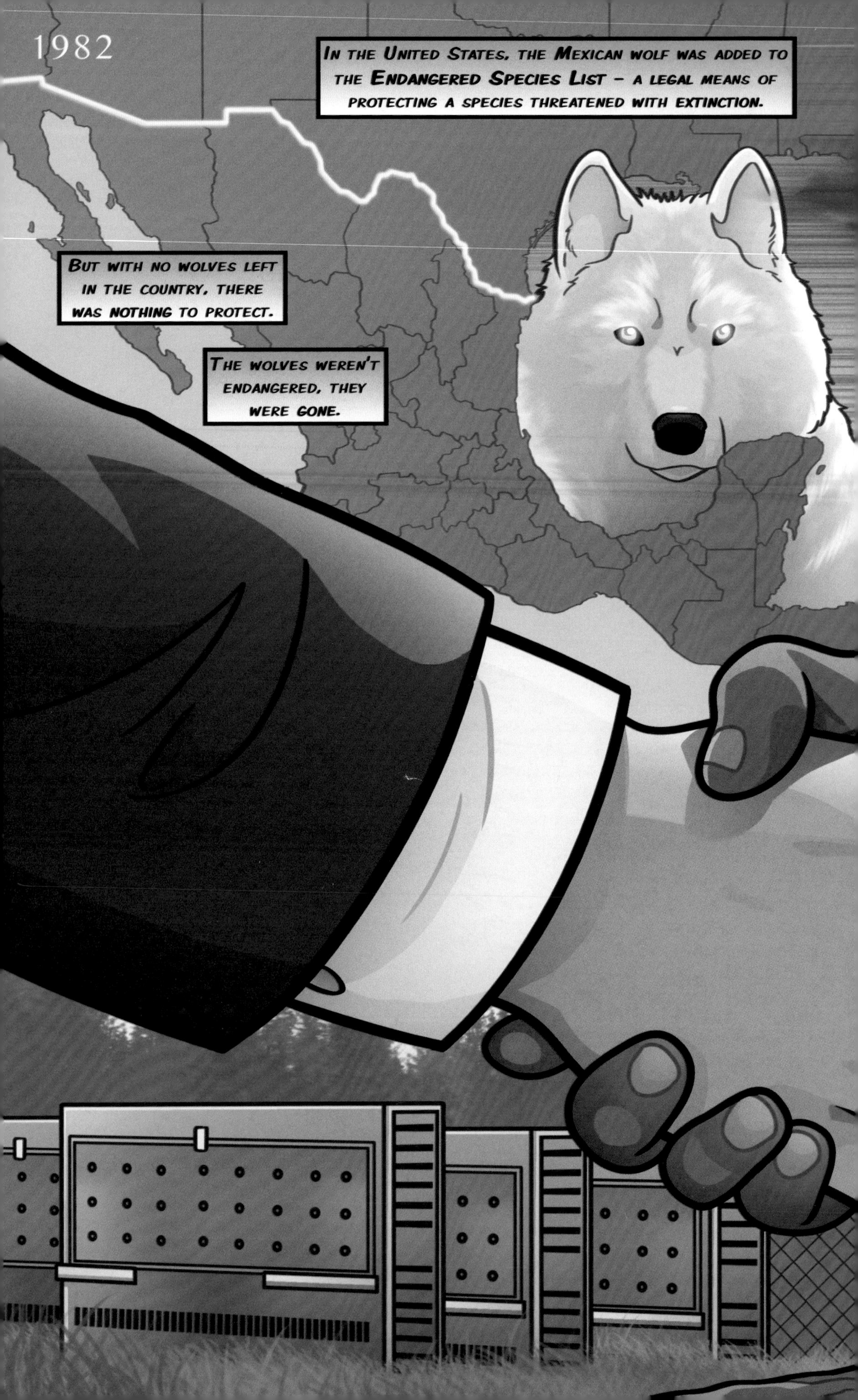
1982
In the United States, the Mexican wolf was added to the Endangered Species List – a legal means of protecting a species threatened with extinction.
But with no wolves left in the country, there was nothing to protect.
The wolves weren't endangered, they were gone.

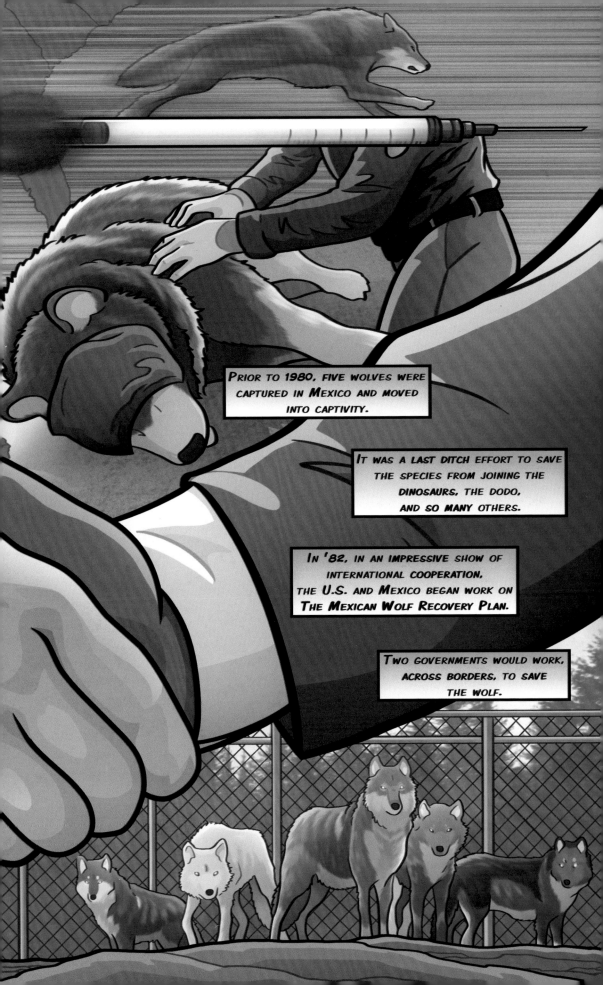

PRIOR TO 1980, FIVE WOLVES WERE CAPTURED IN MEXICO AND MOVED INTO CAPTIVITY.

IT WAS A LAST DITCH EFFORT TO SAVE THE SPECIES FROM JOINING THE DINOSAURS, THE DODO, AND SO MANY OTHERS.

IN '82, IN AN IMPRESSIVE SHOW OF INTERNATIONAL COOPERATION, THE U.S. AND MEXICO BEGAN WORK ON THE MEXICAN WOLF RECOVERY PLAN.

TWO GOVERNMENTS WOULD WORK, ACROSS BORDERS, TO SAVE THE WOLF.

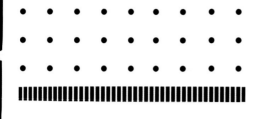

AFTER A SIXTEEN-YEAR CAPTIVE-BREEDING PROGRAM, A SMALL NUMBER OF MEXICAN WOLVES WERE RELEASED NORTH OF THE BORDER.

FOR THE FIRST TIME IN A VERY LONG TIME —

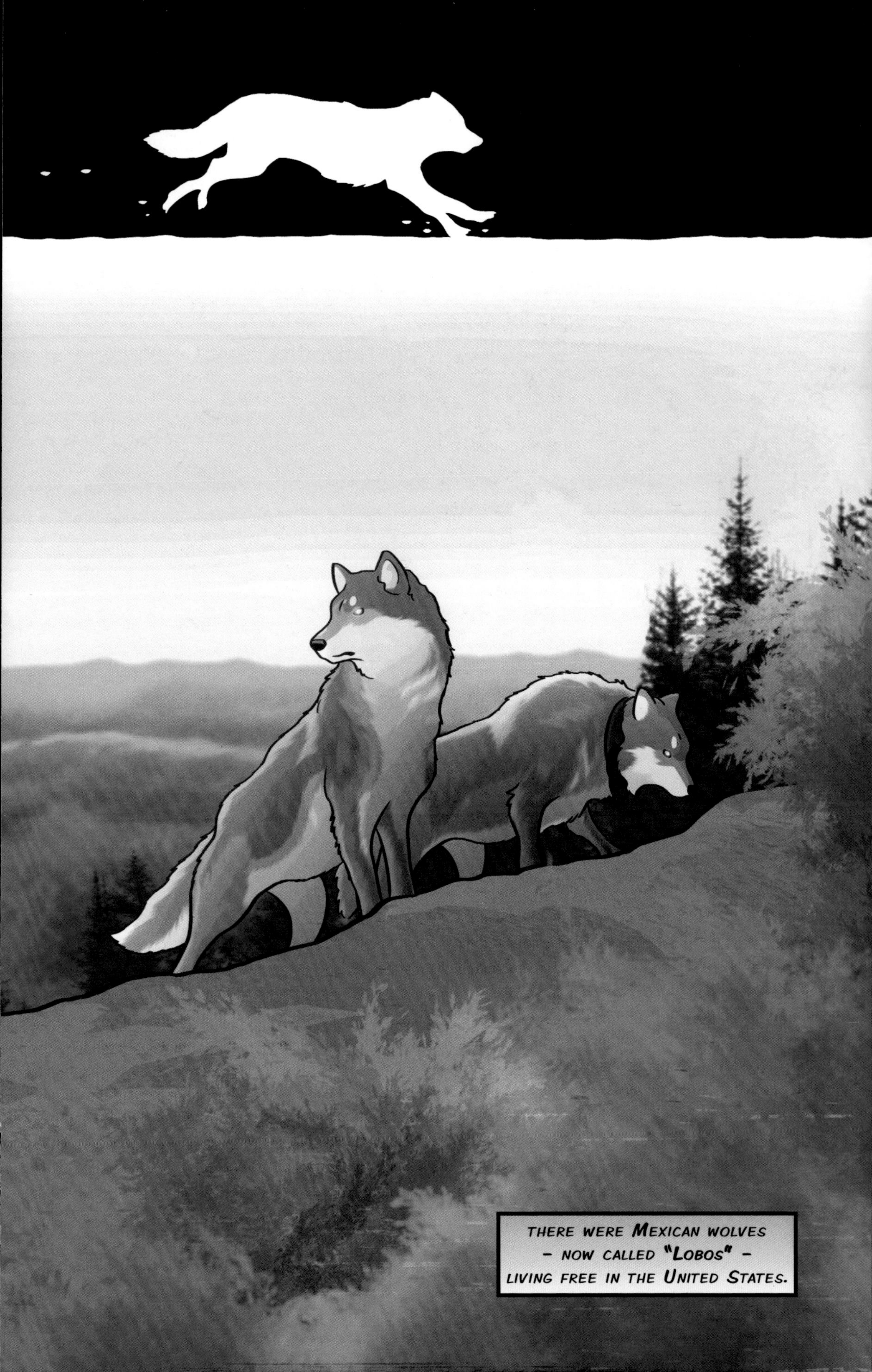
THERE WERE MEXICAN WOLVES
– NOW CALLED "LOBOS" –
LIVING FREE IN THE UNITED STATES.

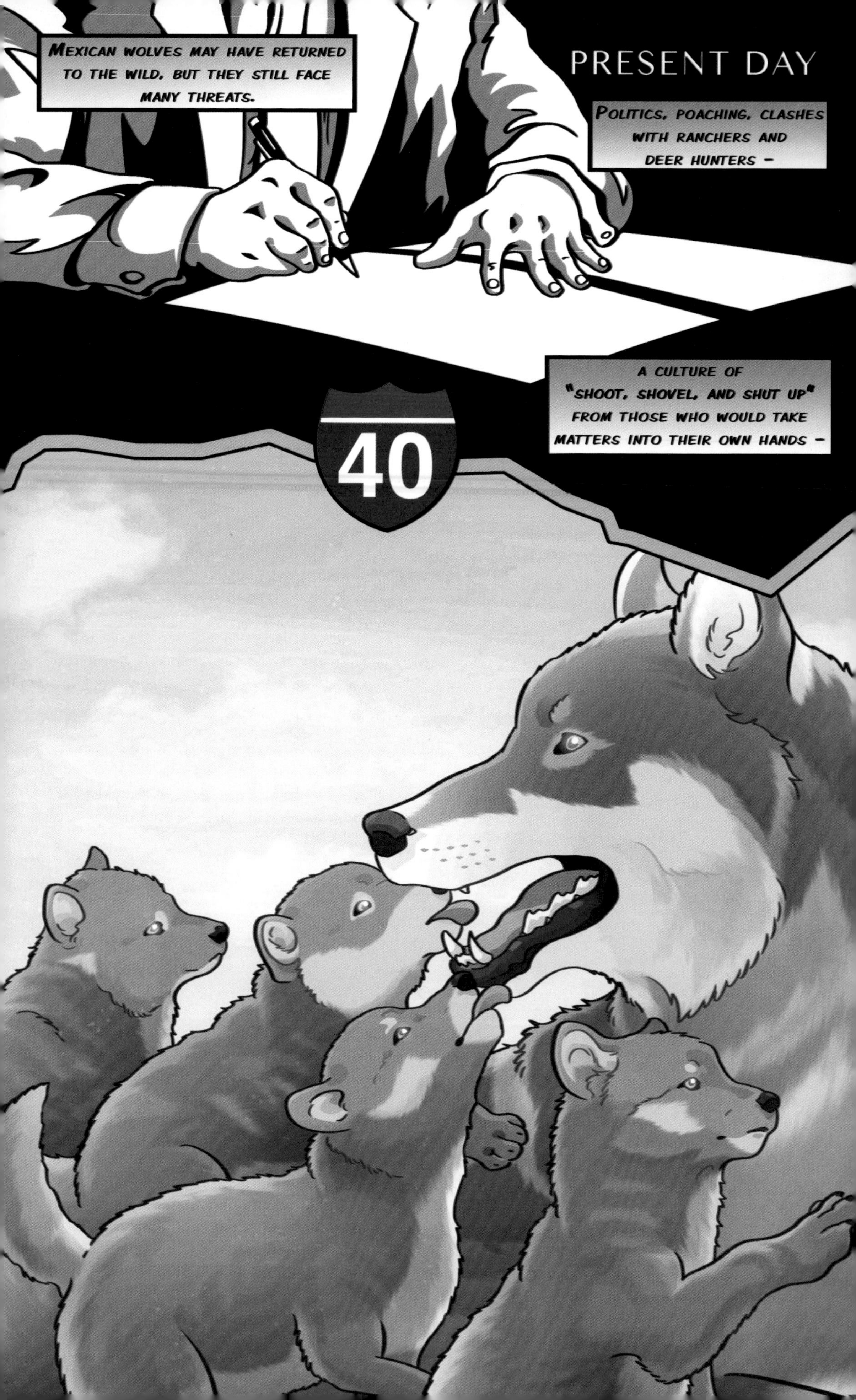
Mexican wolves may have returned to the wild, but they still face many threats.
PRESENT DAY
Politics, poaching, clashes with ranchers and deer hunters –
A culture of "shoot, shovel, and shut up" from those who would take matters into their own hands –
40

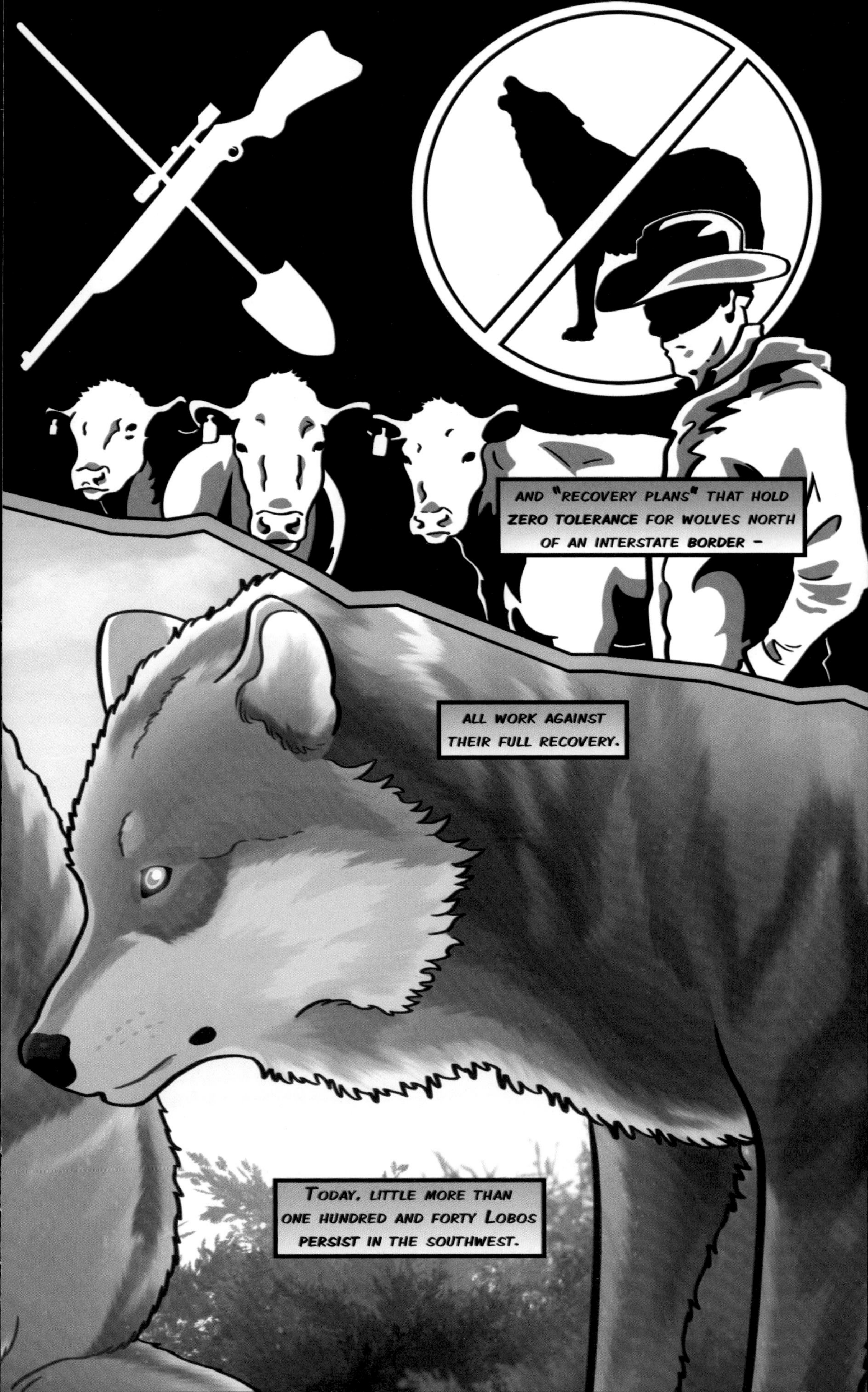
AND "RECOVERY PLANS" THAT HOLD ZERO TOLERANCE FOR WOLVES NORTH OF AN INTERSTATE BORDER –
ALL WORK AGAINST THEIR FULL RECOVERY.
TODAY, LITTLE MORE THAN ONE HUNDRED AND FORTY LOBOS PERSIST IN THE SOUTHWEST.

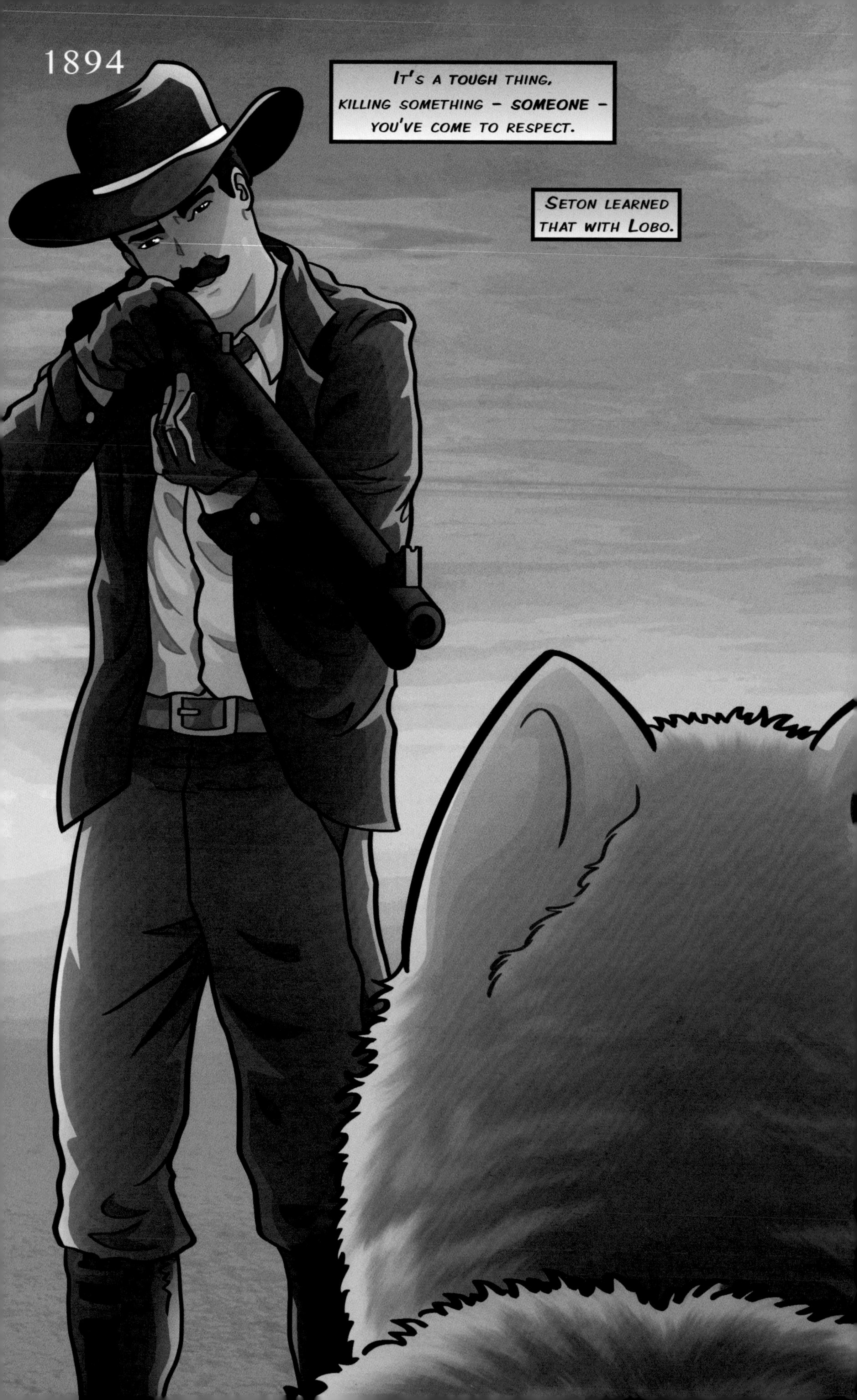
1894
IT'S A TOUGH THING, KILLING SOMETHING - SOMEONE - YOU'VE COME TO RESPECT.
SETON LEARNED THAT WITH LOBO.

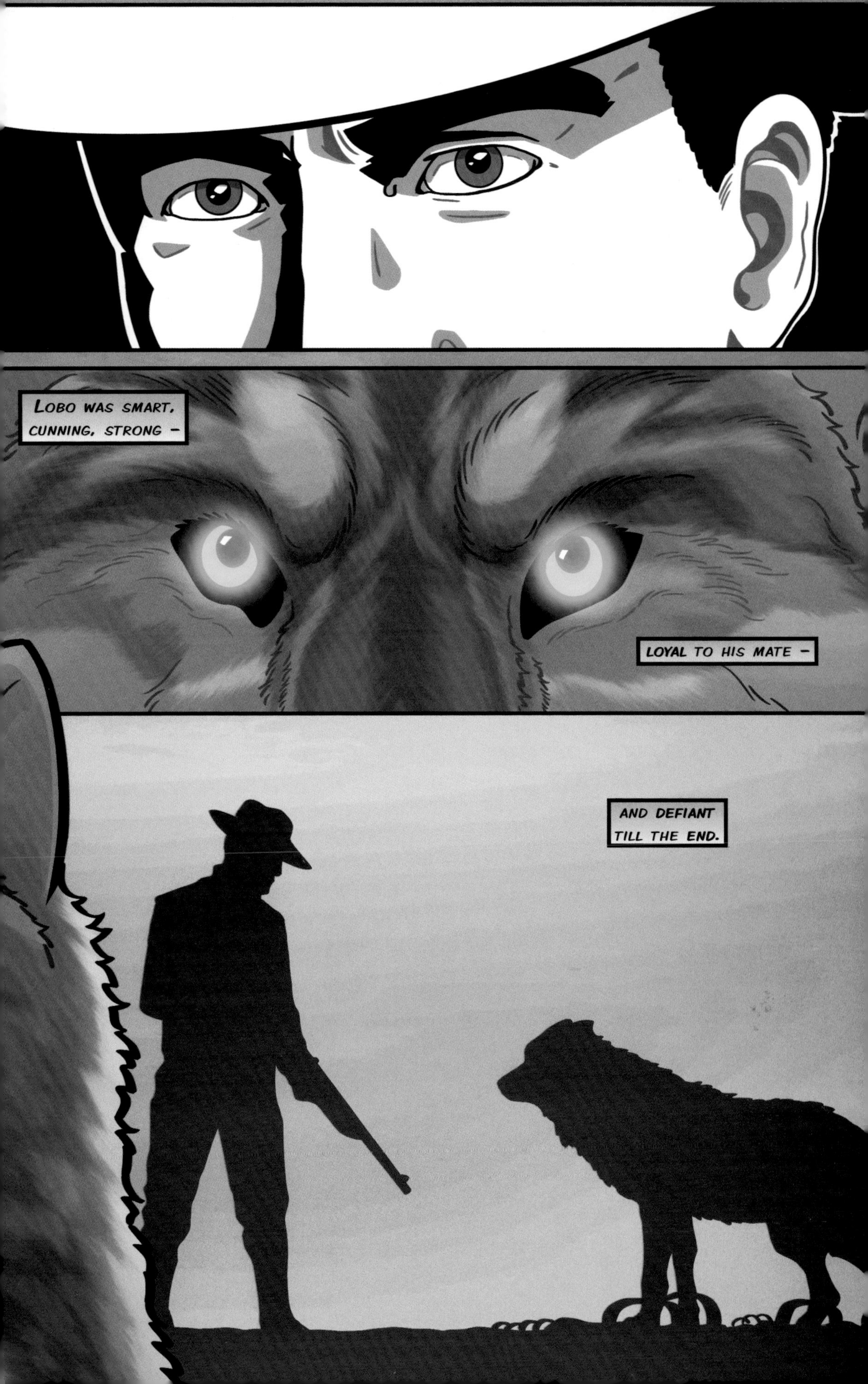
LOBO WAS SMART, CUNNING, STRONG -
LOYAL TO HIS MATE -
AND DEFIANT TILL THE END.

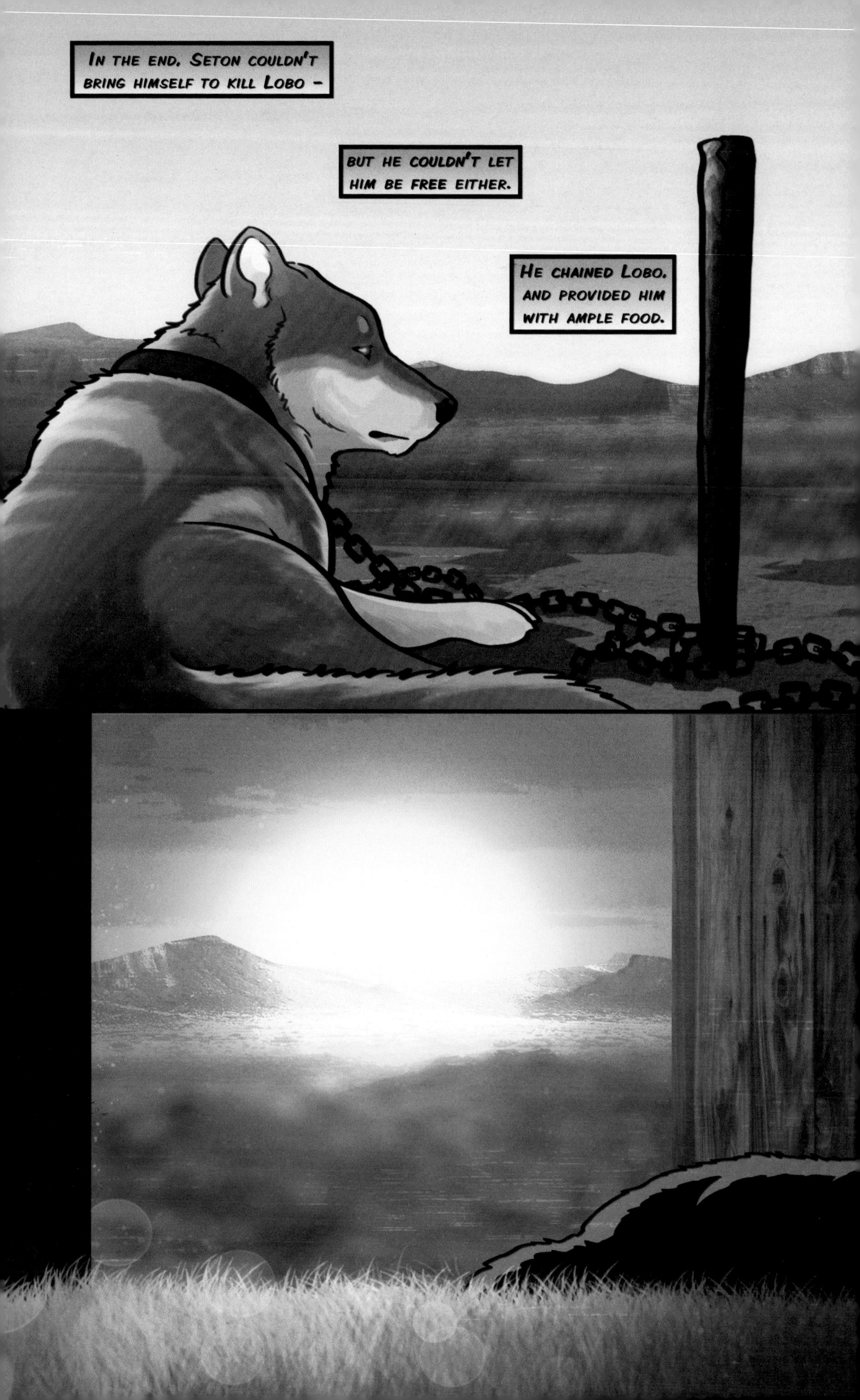
In the end, Seton couldn't bring himself to kill Lobo –
But he couldn't let him be free either.
He chained Lobo, and provided him with ample food.

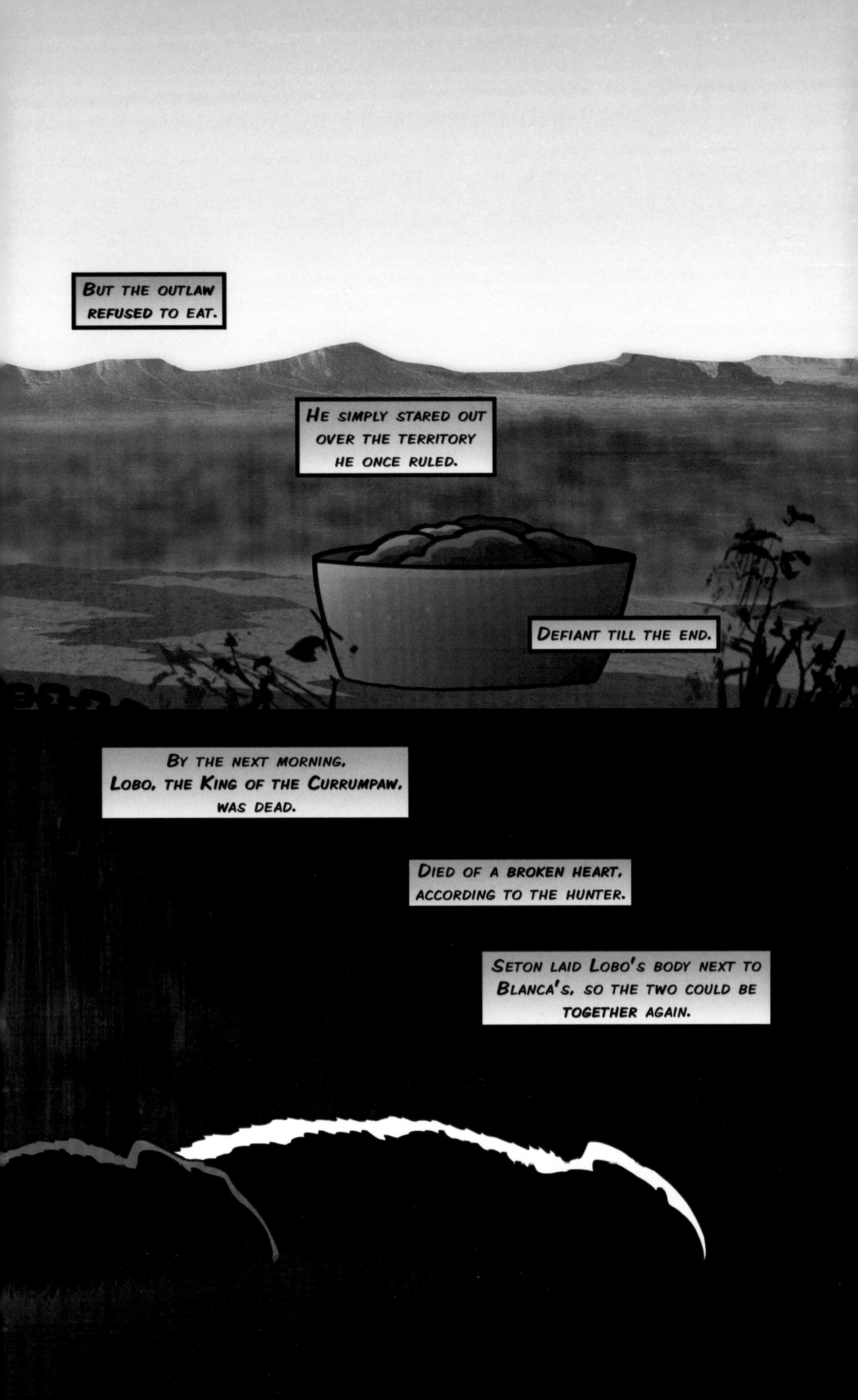

But the outlaw refused to eat.
He simply stared out over the territory he once ruled.
Defiant till the end.
By the next morning, Lobo, the King of the Currumpaw, was dead.
Died of a broken heart, according to the hunter.
Seton laid Lobo's body next to Blanca's, so the two could be together again.

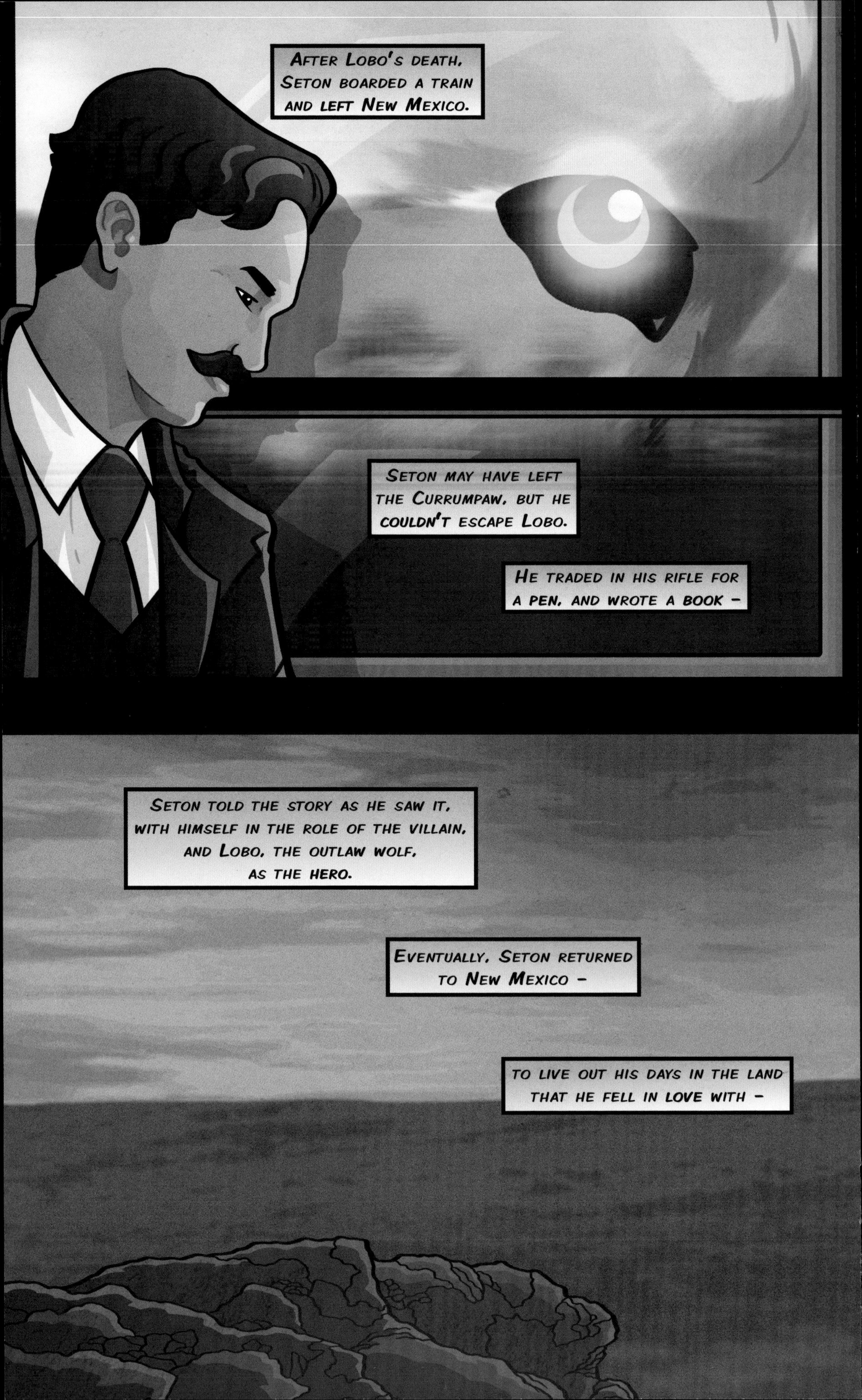
AFTER LOBO'S DEATH, SETON BOARDED A TRAIN AND LEFT NEW MEXICO.
SETON MAY HAVE LEFT THE CURRUMPAW, BUT HE COULDN'T ESCAPE LOBO.
HE TRADED IN HIS RIFLE FOR A PEN, AND WROTE A BOOK –
SETON TOLD THE STORY AS HE SAW IT, WITH HIMSELF IN THE ROLE OF THE VILLAIN, AND LOBO, THE OUTLAW WOLF, AS THE HERO.
EVENTUALLY, SETON RETURNED TO NEW MEXICO –
TO LIVE OUT HIS DAYS IN THE LAND THAT HE FELL IN LOVE WITH –

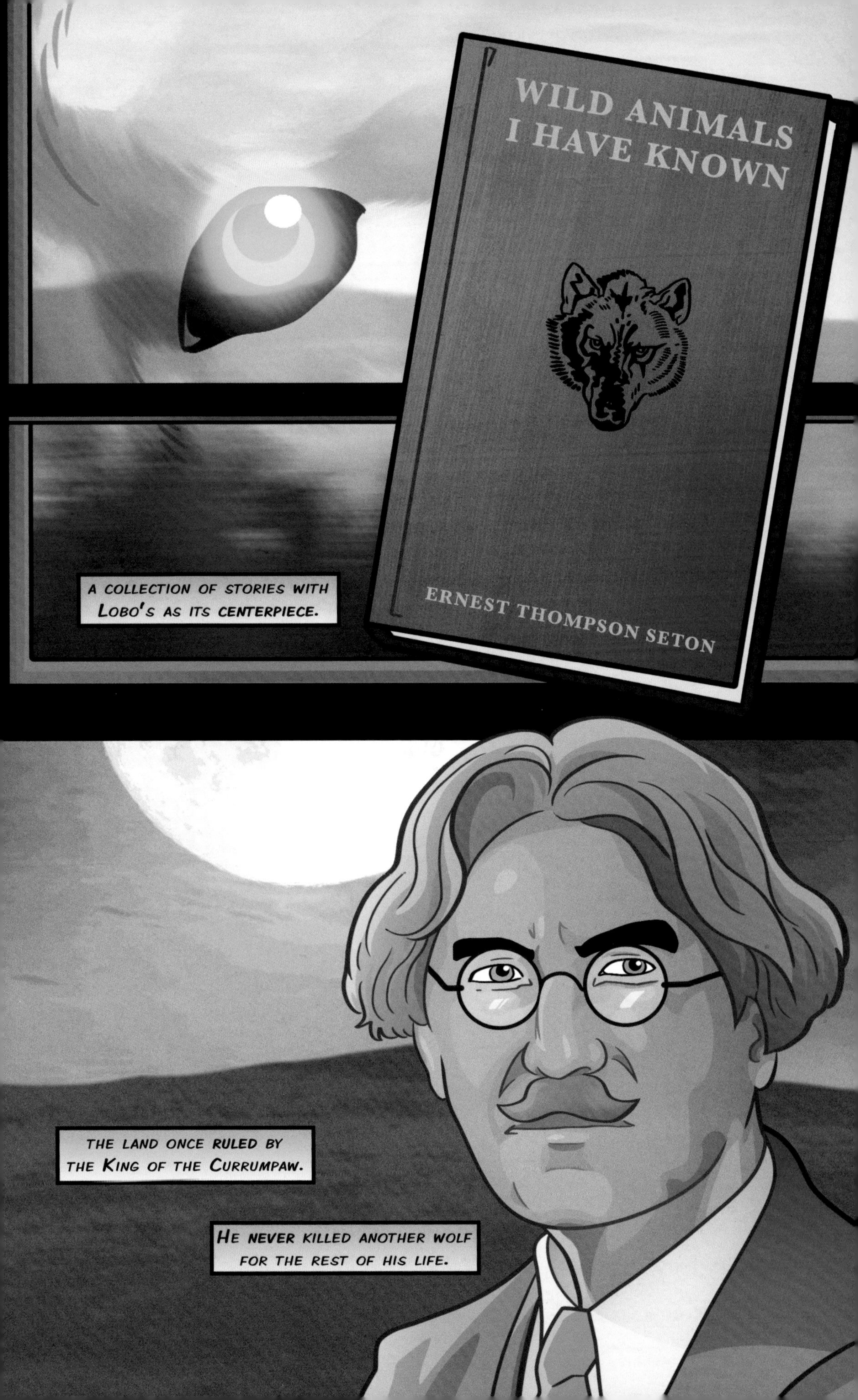
WILD ANIMALS I HAVE KNOWN
ERNEST THOMPSON SETON
A COLLECTION OF STORIES WITH LOBO'S AS ITS CENTERPIECE.
THE LAND ONCE RULED BY THE KING OF THE CURRUMPAW.
HE NEVER KILLED ANOTHER WOLF FOR THE REST OF HIS LIFE.

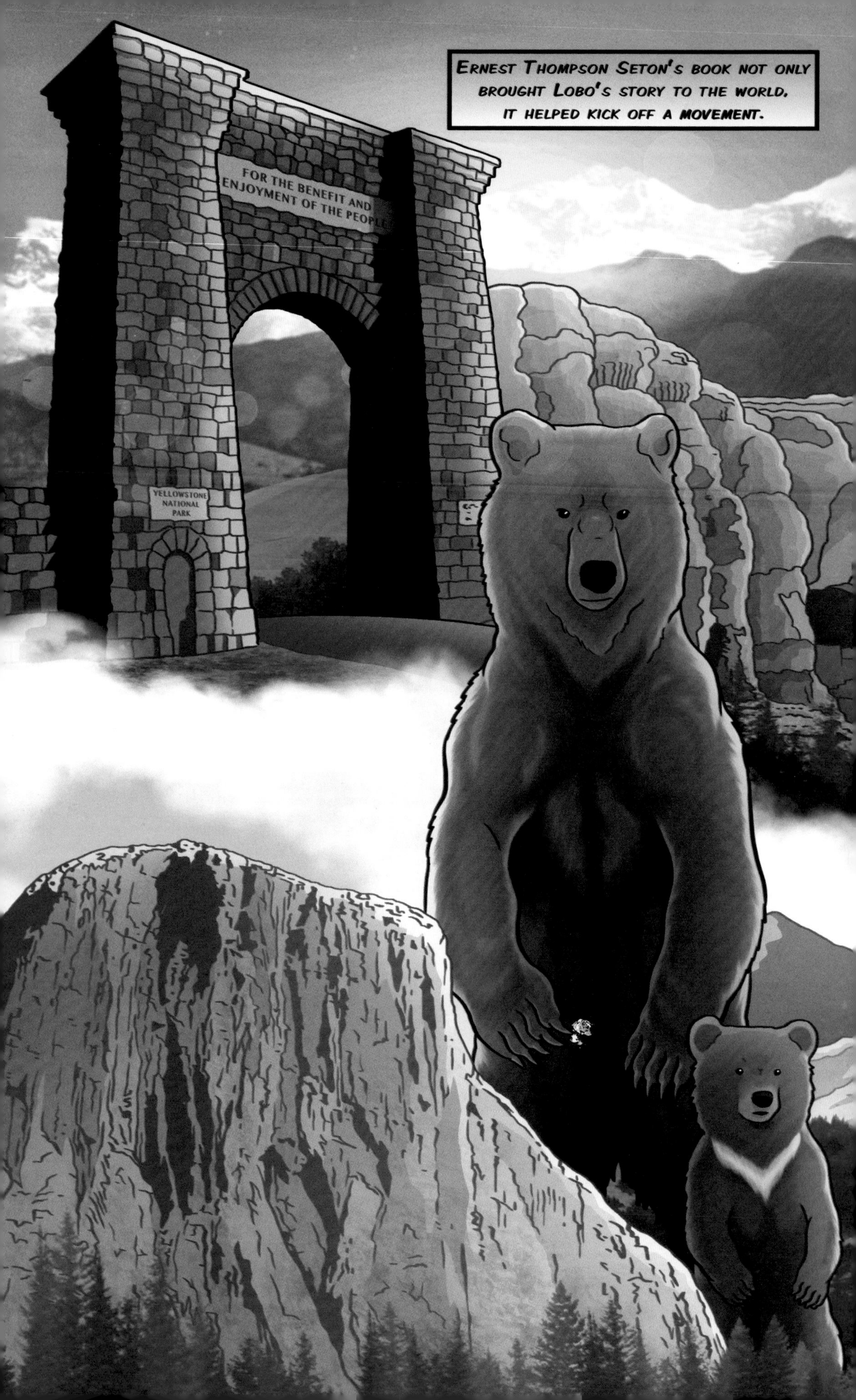
ERNEST THOMPSON SETON'S BOOK NOT ONLY BROUGHT LOBO'S STORY TO THE WORLD, IT HELPED KICK OFF A MOVEMENT.
FOR THE BENEFIT AND ENJOYMENT OF THE PEOPLE
YELLOWSTONE NATIONAL PARK

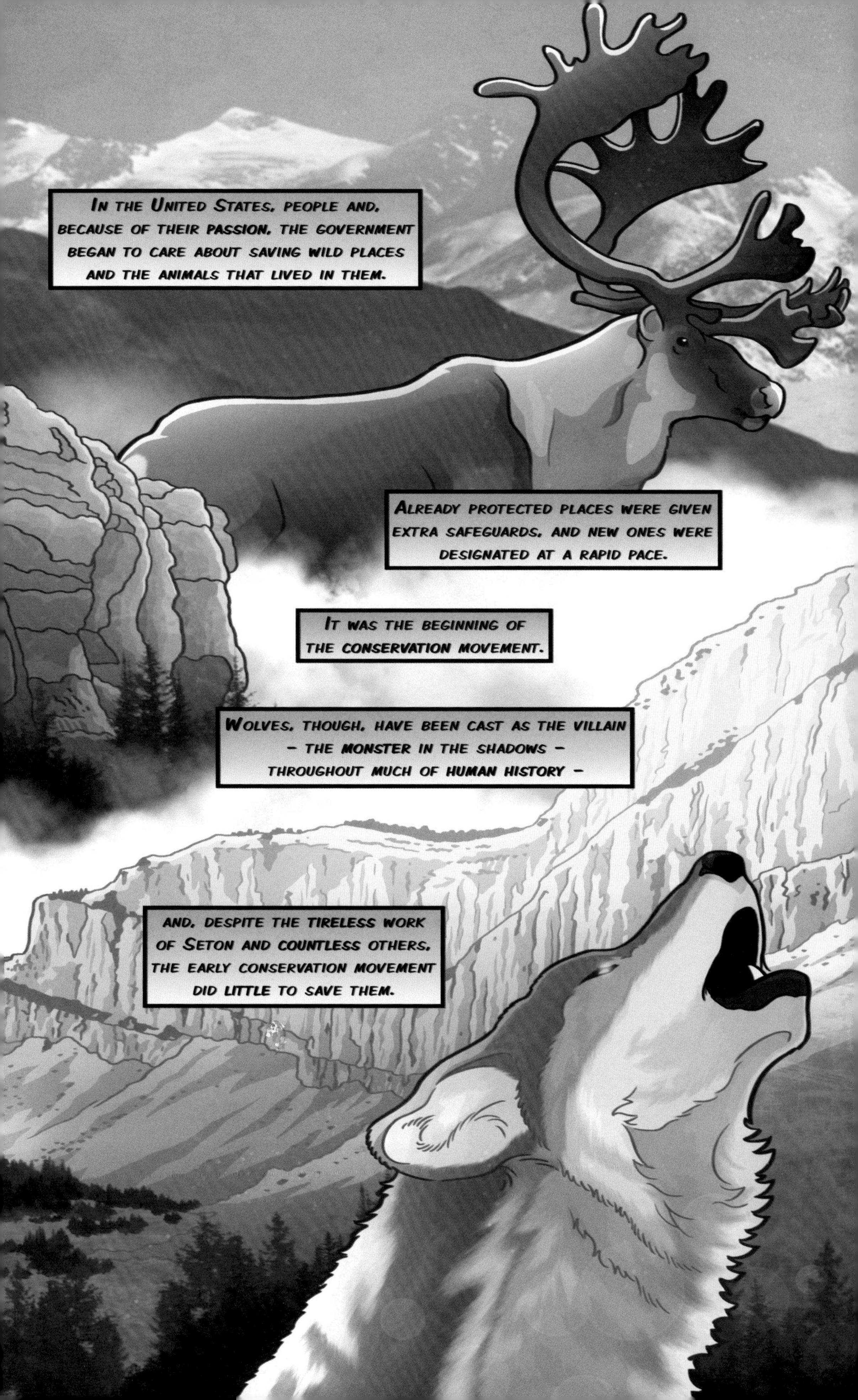
In the United States, people and, because of their passion, the government began to care about saving wild places and the animals that lived in them.
Already protected places were given extra safeguards, and new ones were designated at a rapid pace.
It was the beginning of the conservation movement.
Wolves, though, have been cast as the villain – the monster in the shadows – throughout much of human history –
and, despite the tireless work of Seton and countless others, the early conservation movement did little to save them.

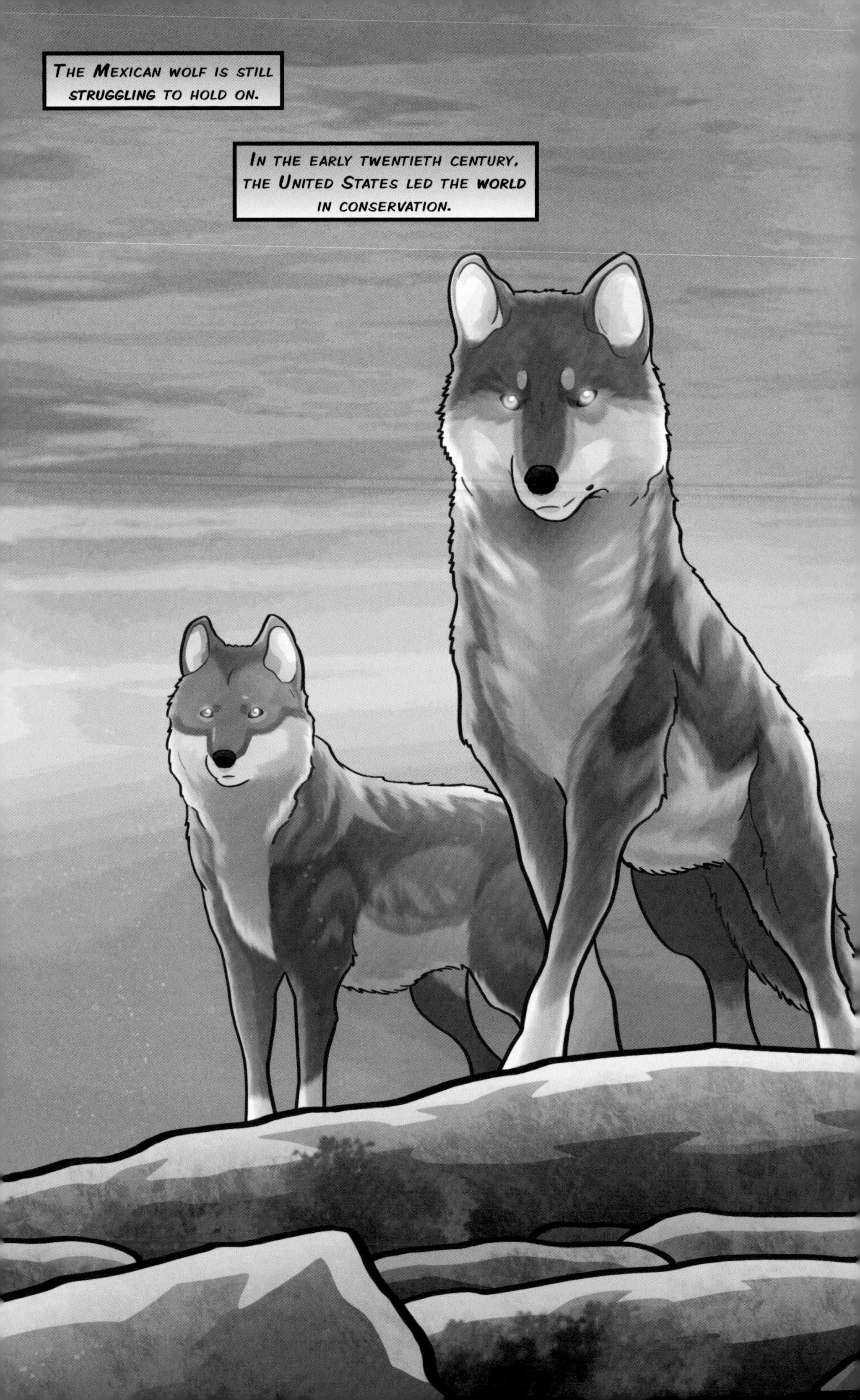
The Mexican wolf is still struggling to hold on.
In the early twentieth century, the United States led the world in conservation.

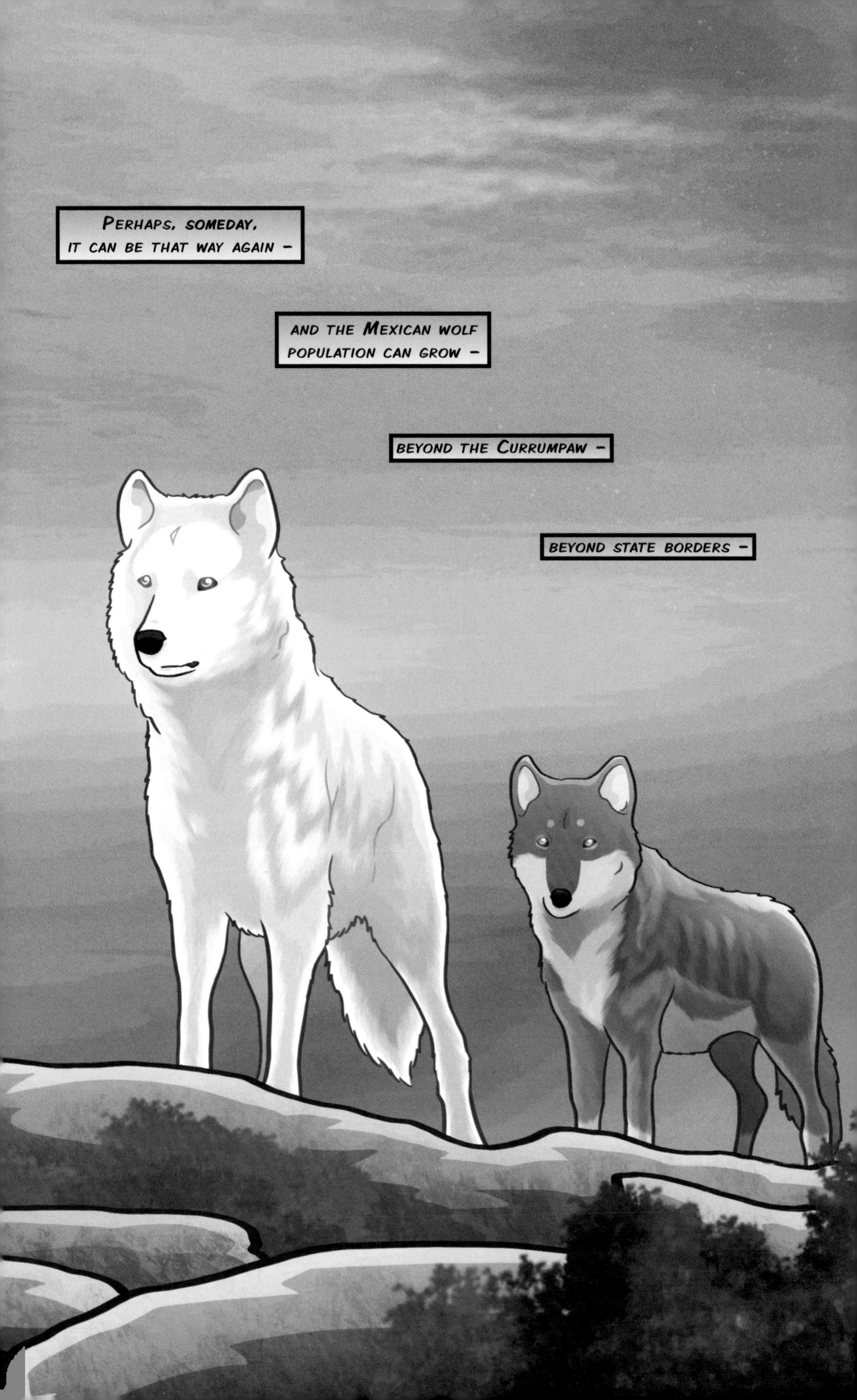
PERHAPS, SOMEDAY, IT CAN BE THAT WAY AGAIN –
AND THE MEXICAN WOLF POPULATION CAN GROW –
BEYOND THE CURRUMPAW –
BEYOND STATE BORDERS –

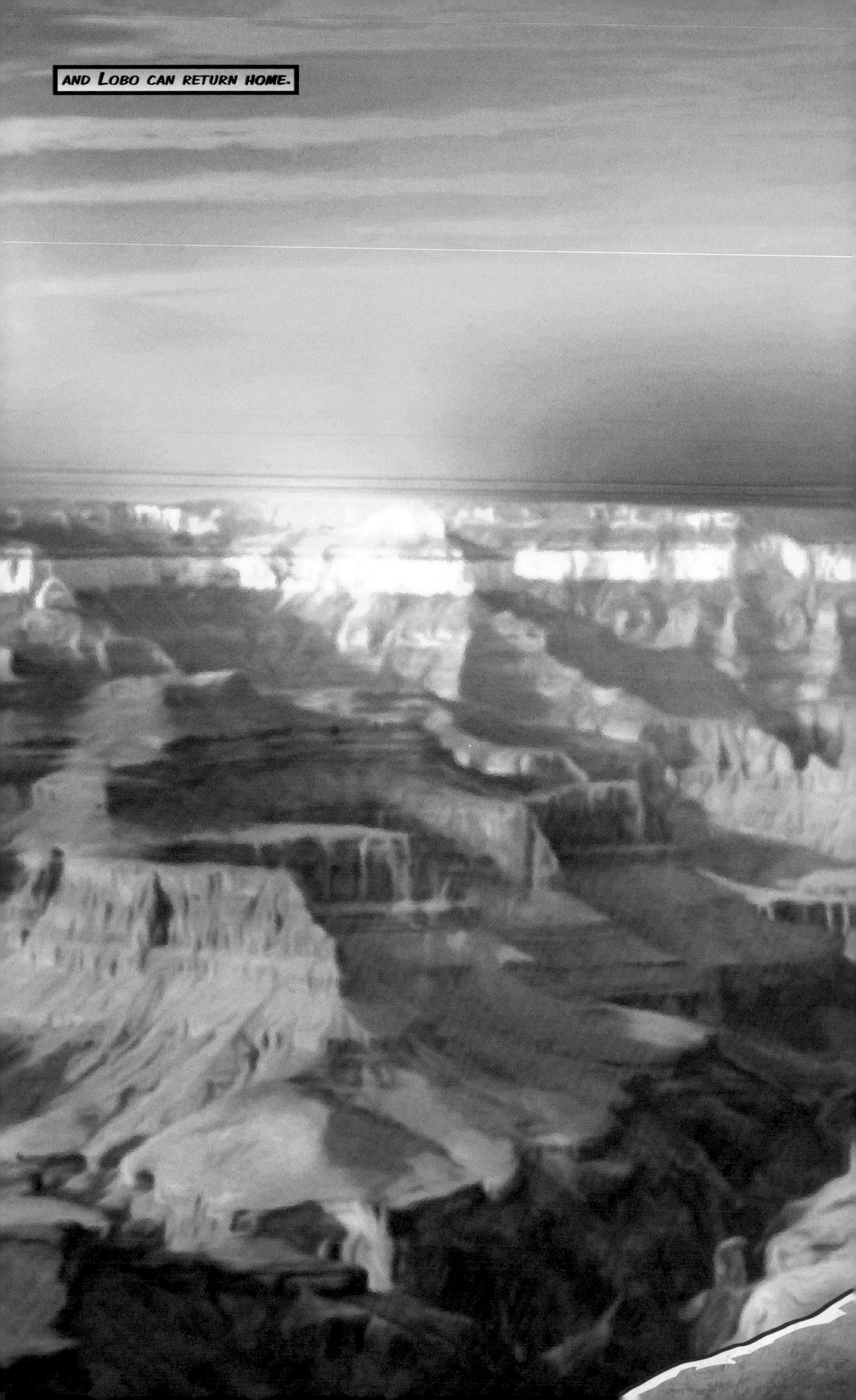
AND LOBO CAN RETURN HOME.

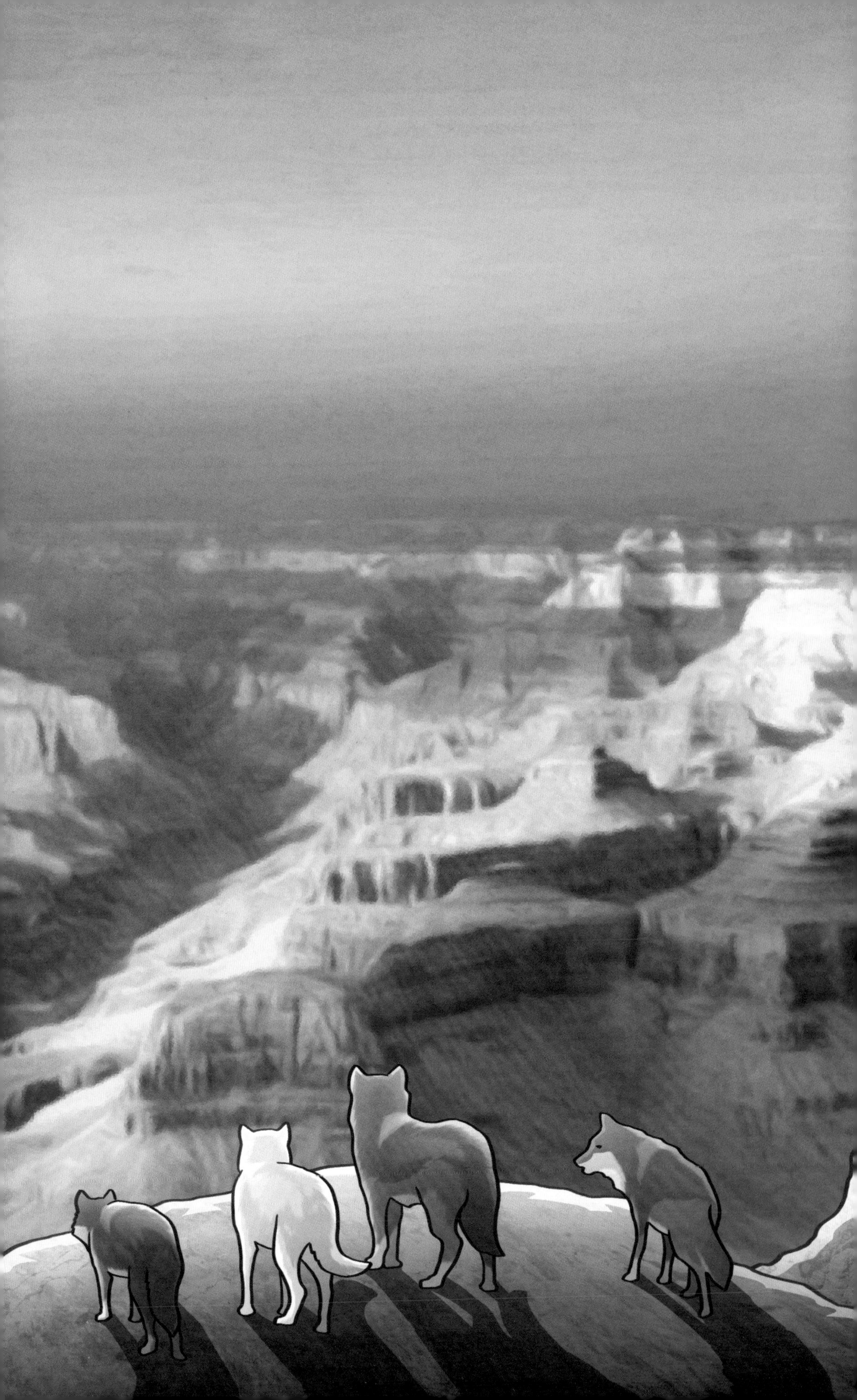

21

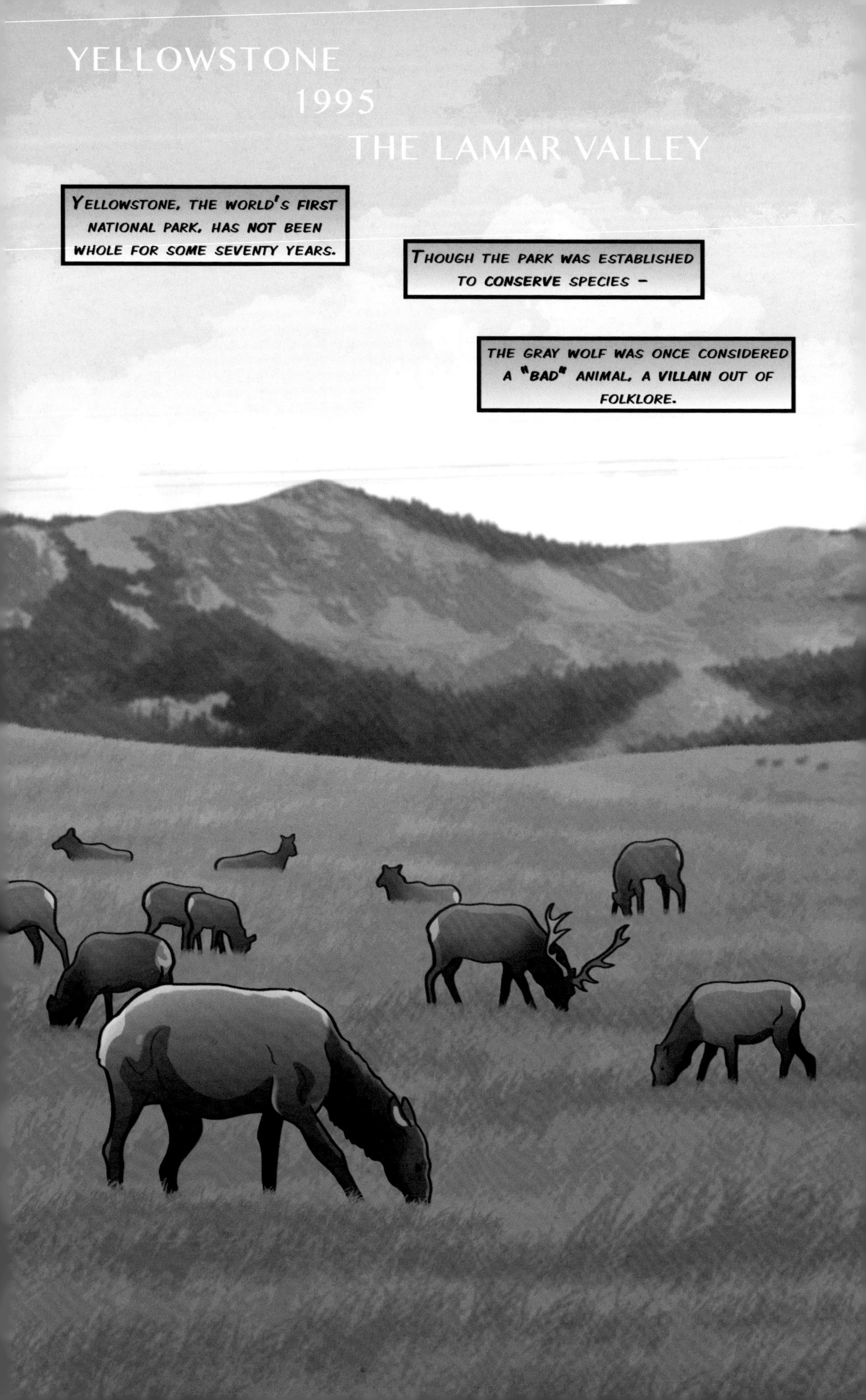
YELLOWSTONE
1995
THE LAMAR VALLEY
YELLOWSTONE, THE WORLD'S FIRST NATIONAL PARK, HAS NOT BEEN WHOLE FOR SOME SEVENTY YEARS.
THOUGH THE PARK WAS ESTABLISHED TO CONSERVE SPECIES –
THE GRAY WOLF WAS ONCE CONSIDERED A "BAD" ANIMAL, A VILLAIN OUT OF FOLKLORE.

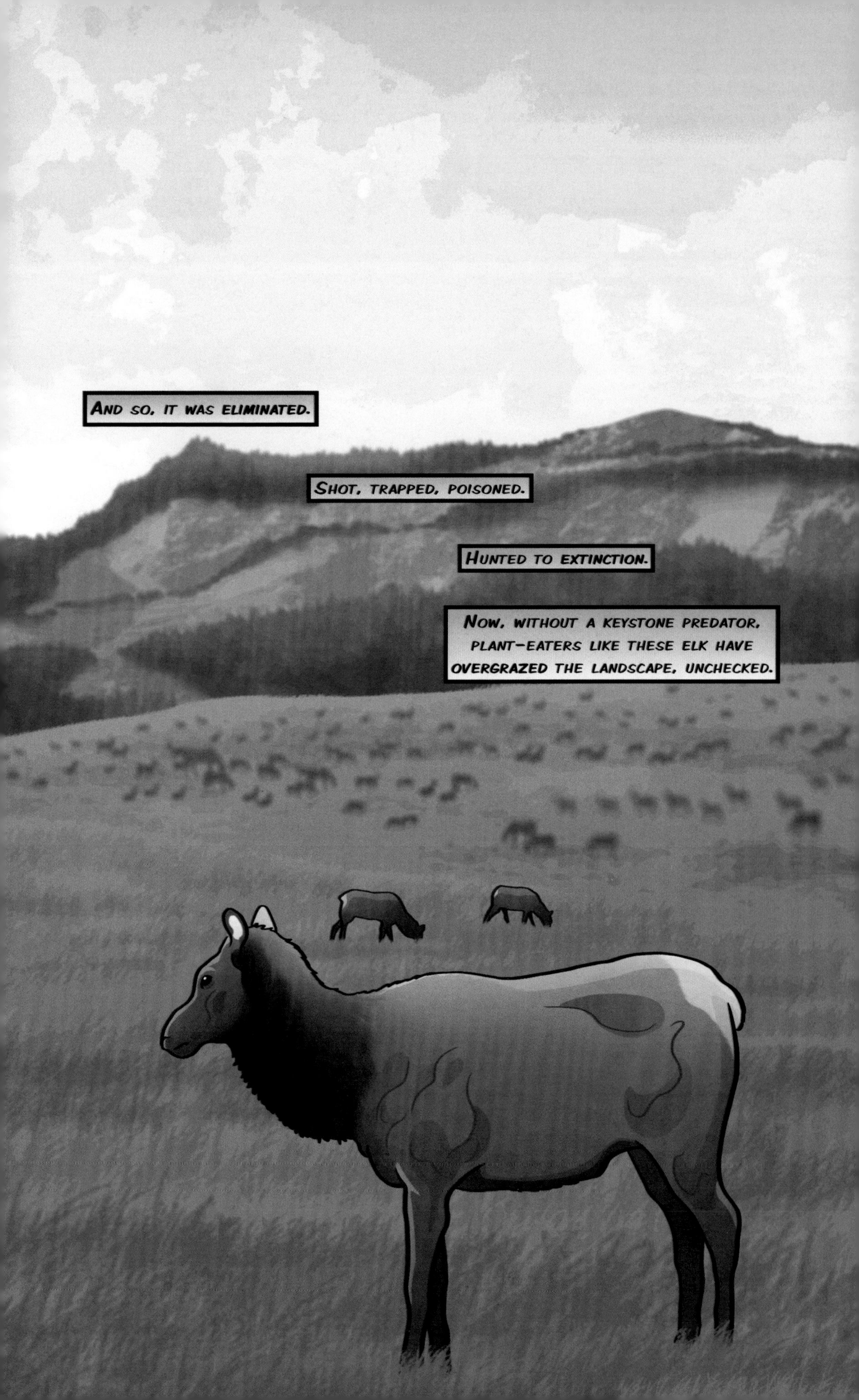
And so, it was eliminated.
Shot, trapped, poisoned.
Hunted to extinction.
Now, without a keystone predator, plant-eaters like these elk have overgrazed the landscape, unchecked.

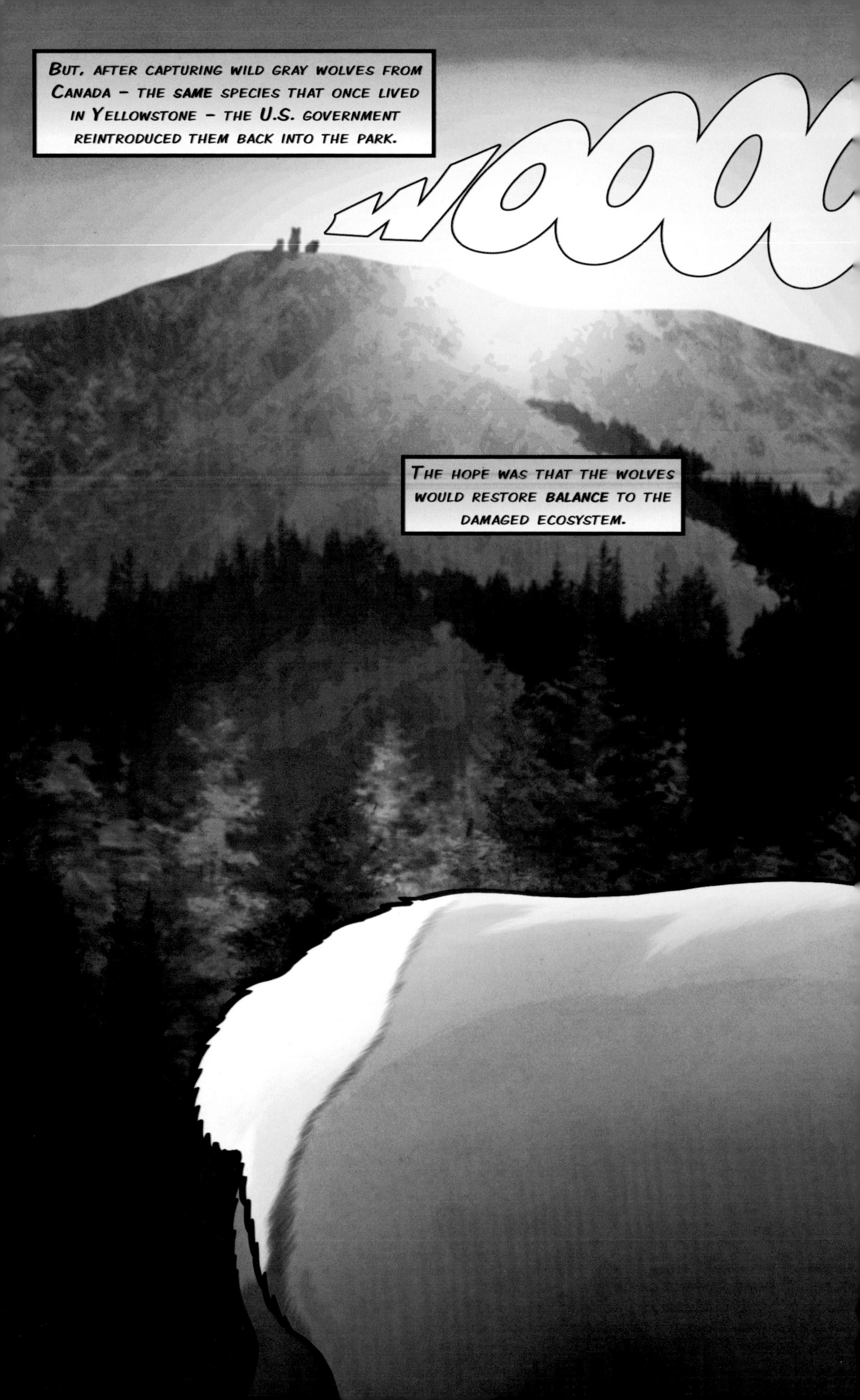
But, after capturing wild gray wolves from Canada – the same species that once lived in Yellowstone – the U.S. government reintroduced them back into the park.
WOOO
The hope was that the wolves would restore balance to the damaged ecosystem.

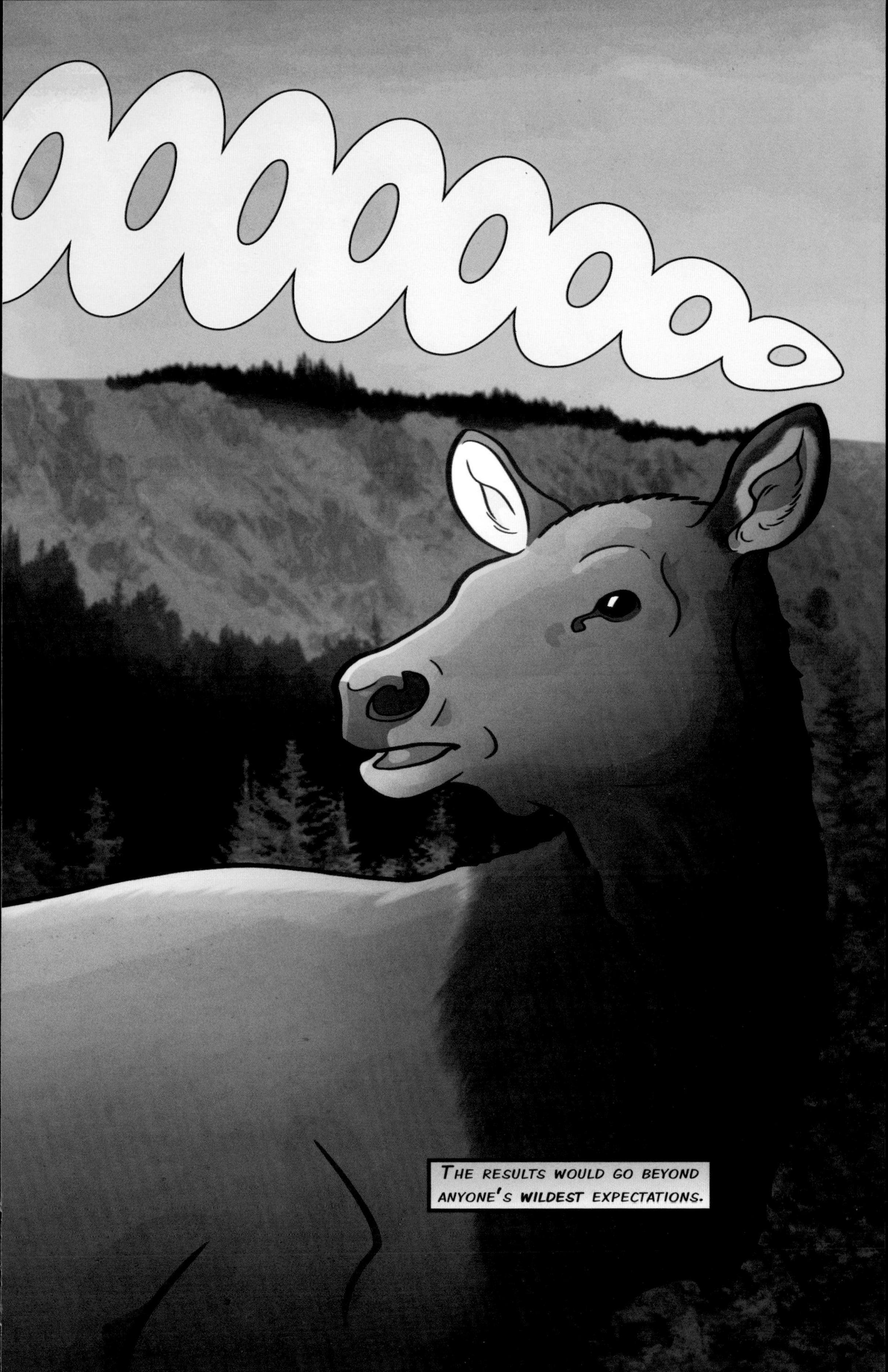
OOOOOOOOO
THE RESULTS WOULD GO BEYOND ANYONE'S WILDEST EXPECTATIONS.

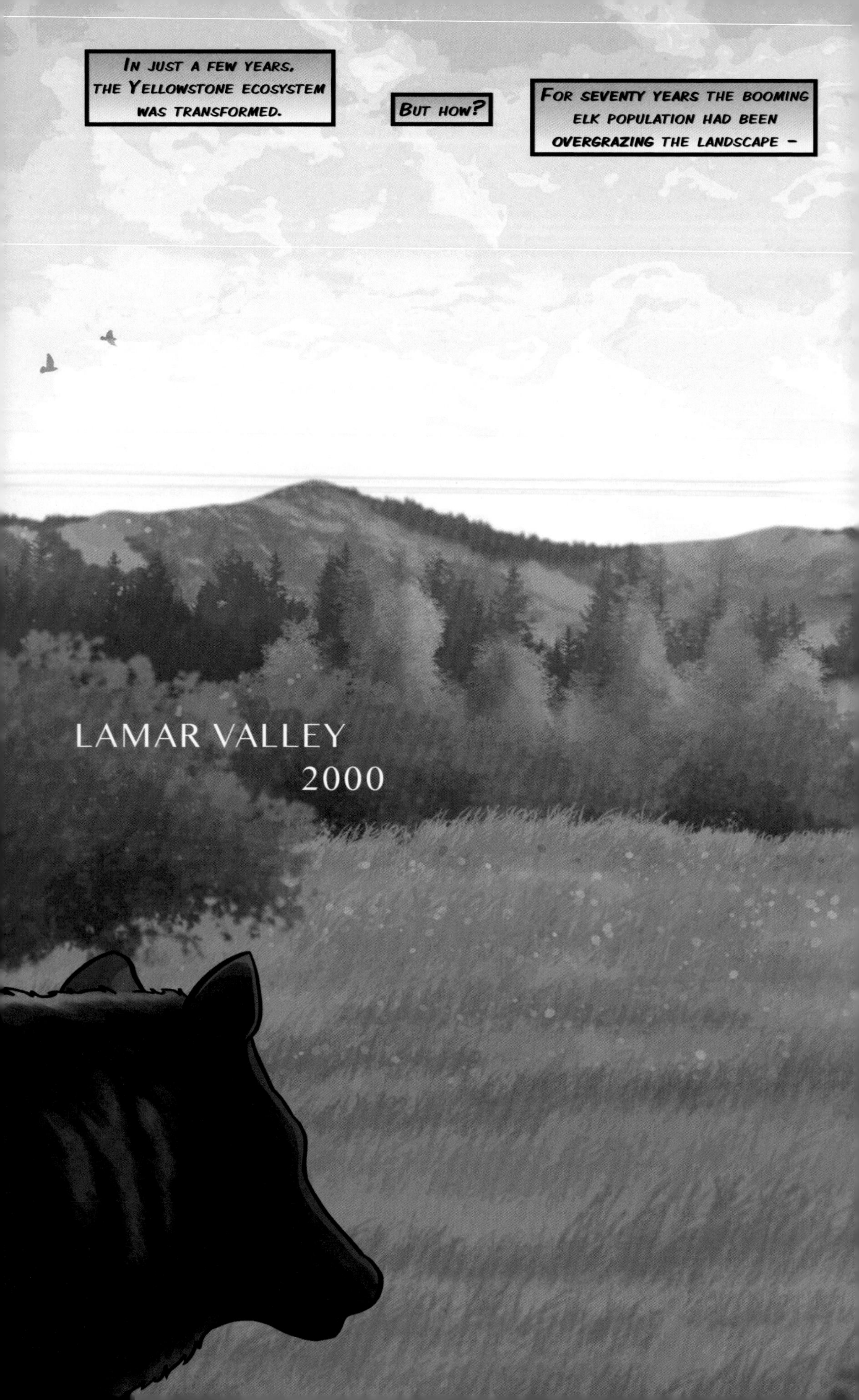
In just a few years, the Yellowstone ecosystem was transformed.
But how?
For seventy years the booming elk population had been overgrazing the landscape –
LAMAR VALLEY 2000

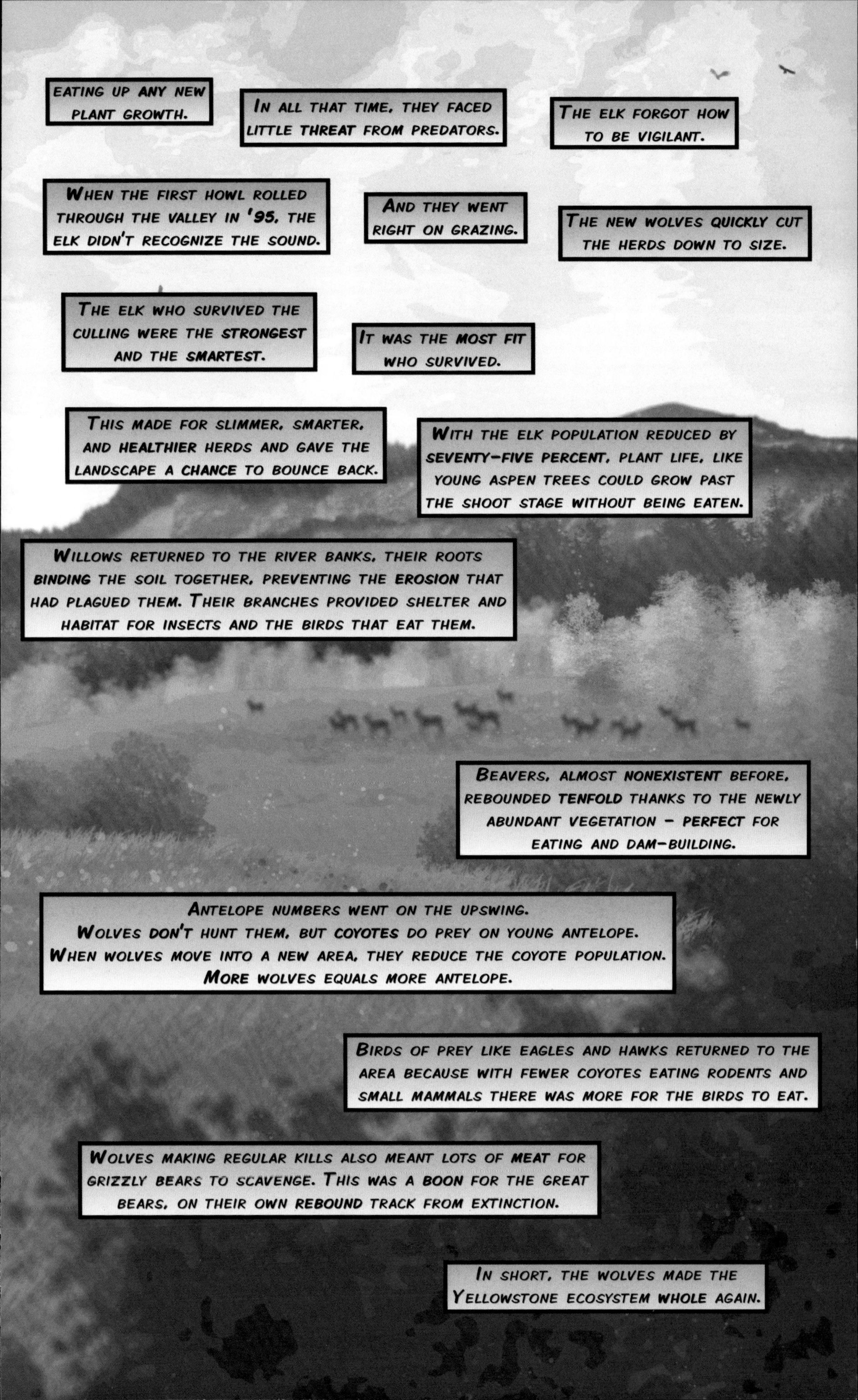
eating up any new plant growth.
In all that time, they faced little threat from predators.
The elk forgot how to be vigilant.
When the first howl rolled through the valley in '95, the elk didn't recognize the sound.
And they went right on grazing.
The new wolves quickly cut the herds down to size.
The elk who survived the culling were the strongest and the smartest.
It was the most fit who survived.
This made for slimmer, smarter, and healthier herds and gave the landscape a chance to bounce back.
With the elk population reduced by seventy-five percent, plant life, like young aspen trees could grow past the shoot stage without being eaten.
Willows returned to the river banks, their roots binding the soil together, preventing the erosion that had plagued them. Their branches provided shelter and habitat for insects and the birds that eat them.
Beavers, almost nonexistent before, rebounded tenfold thanks to the newly abundant vegetation – perfect for eating and dam-building.
Antelope numbers went on the upswing. Wolves don't hunt them, but coyotes do prey on young antelope. When wolves move into a new area, they reduce the coyote population. More wolves equals more antelope.
Birds of prey like eagles and hawks returned to the area because with fewer coyotes eating rodents and small mammals there was more for the birds to eat.
Wolves making regular kills also meant lots of meat for grizzly bears to scavenge. This was a boon for the great bears, on their own rebound track from extinction.
In short, the wolves made the Yellowstone ecosystem whole again.

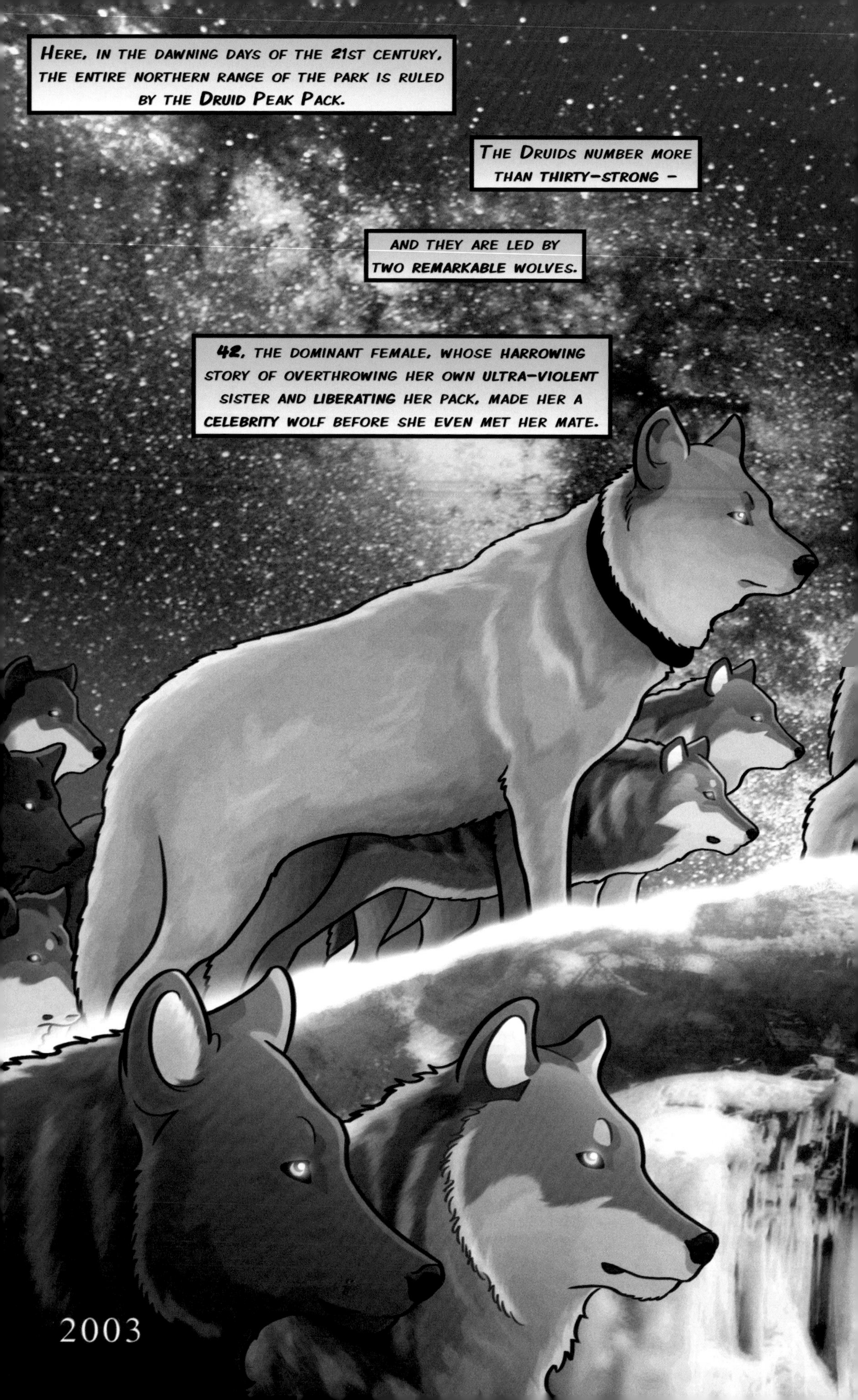
HERE, IN THE DAWNING DAYS OF THE 21ST CENTURY, THE ENTIRE NORTHERN RANGE OF THE PARK IS RULED BY THE DRUID PEAK PACK.
THE DRUIDS NUMBER MORE THAN THIRTY-STRONG -
AND THEY ARE LED BY TWO REMARKABLE WOLVES.
42, THE DOMINANT FEMALE, WHOSE HARROWING STORY OF OVERTHROWING HER OWN ULTRA-VIOLENT SISTER AND LIBERATING HER PACK, MADE HER A CELEBRITY WOLF BEFORE SHE EVEN MET HER MATE.
2003

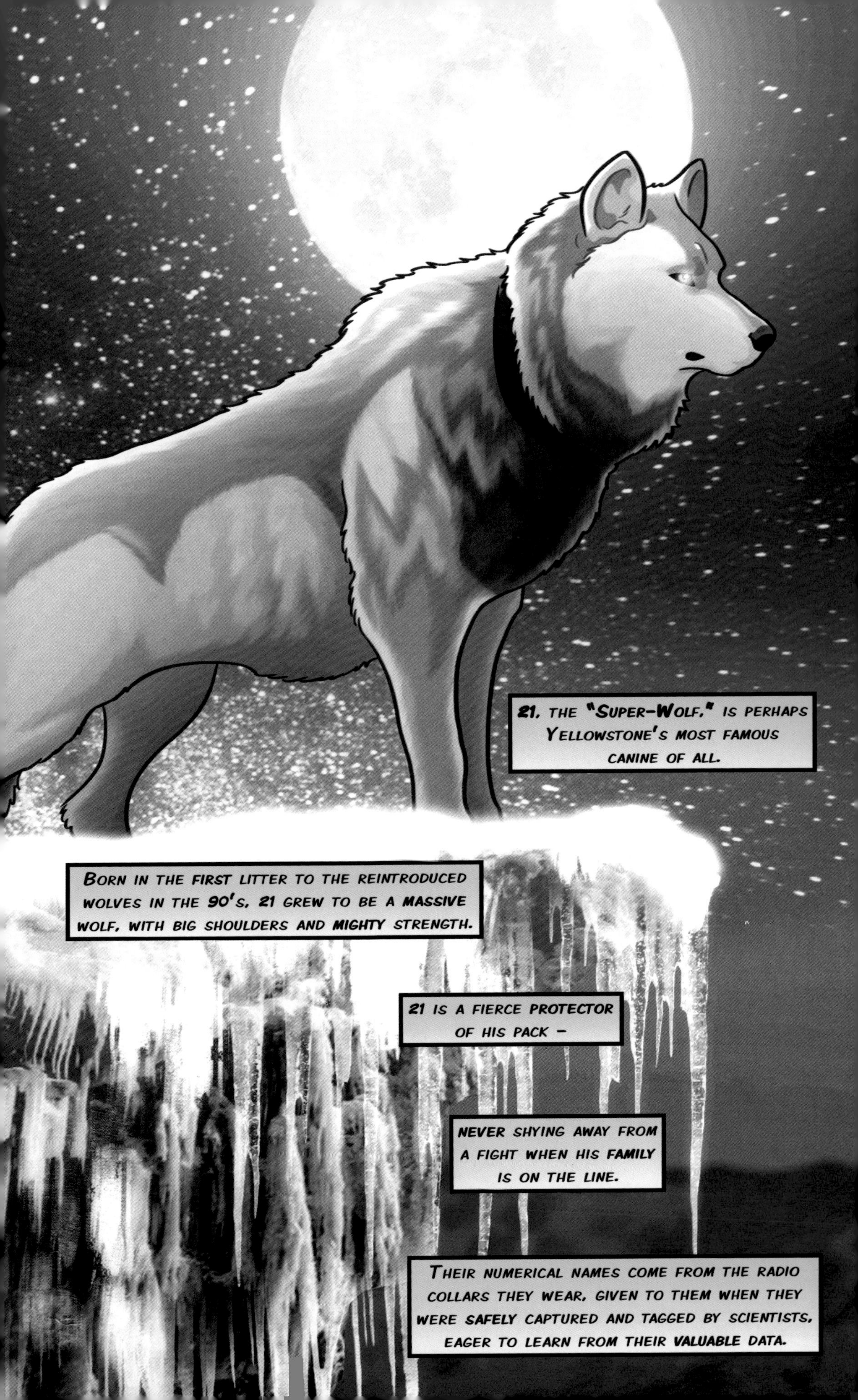
21, THE "SUPER-WOLF," IS PERHAPS YELLOWSTONE'S MOST FAMOUS CANINE OF ALL.
BORN IN THE FIRST LITTER TO THE REINTRODUCED WOLVES IN THE 90'S, 21 GREW TO BE A MASSIVE WOLF, WITH BIG SHOULDERS AND MIGHTY STRENGTH.
21 IS A FIERCE PROTECTOR OF HIS PACK –
NEVER SHYING AWAY FROM A FIGHT WHEN HIS FAMILY IS ON THE LINE.
THEIR NUMERICAL NAMES COME FROM THE RADIO COLLARS THEY WEAR, GIVEN TO THEM WHEN THEY WERE SAFELY CAPTURED AND TAGGED BY SCIENTISTS, EAGER TO LEARN FROM THEIR VALUABLE DATA.

42 AND 21 HAVE BEEN TOGETHER FOR YEARS.

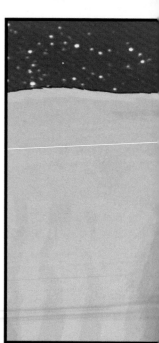

AND, HAVING MADE THE KILL, HE MAKES THE RULES AT MEALTIME.

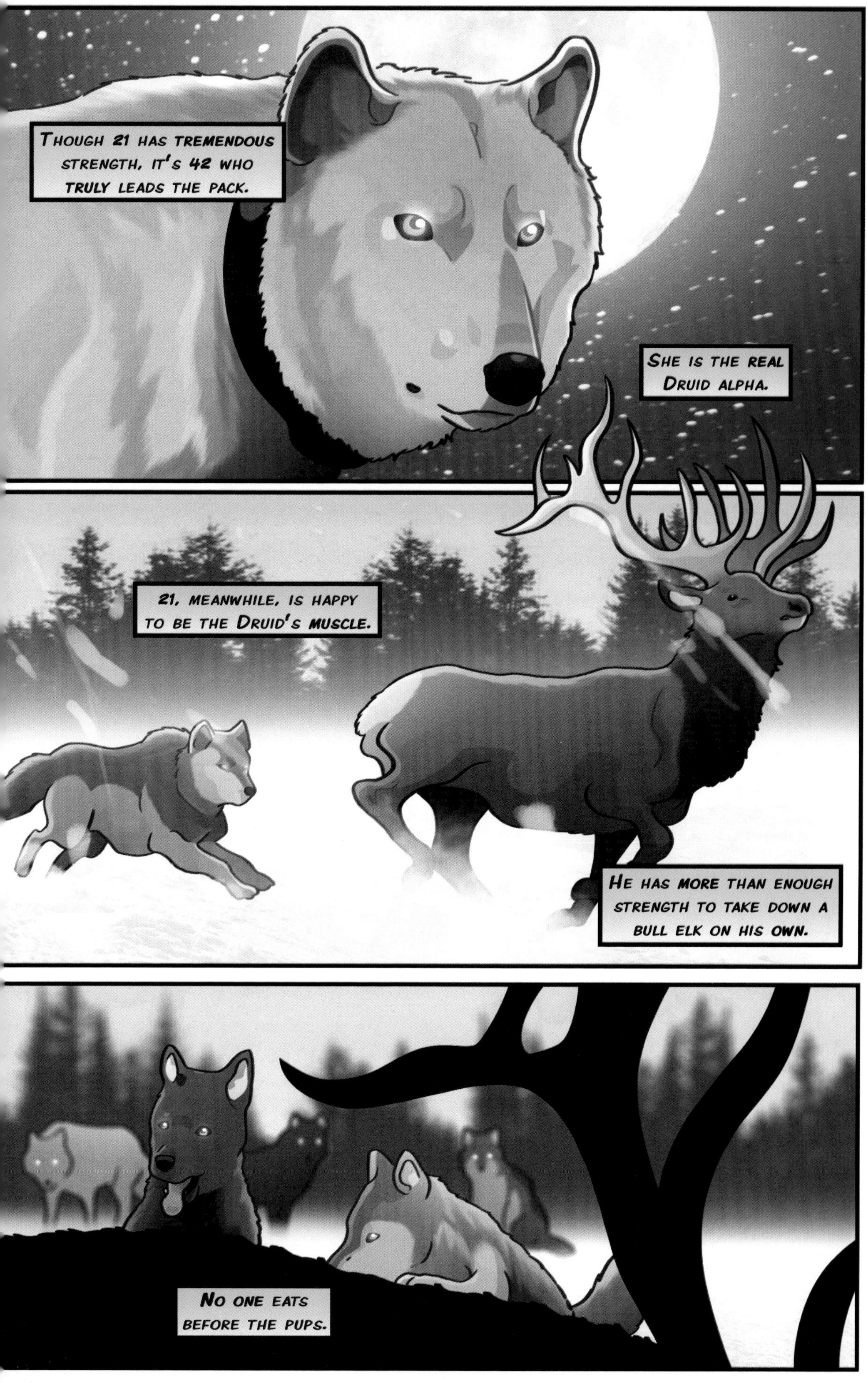
Though 21 has tremendous strength, it's 42 who truly leads the pack.
She is the real Druid alpha.
21, meanwhile, is happy to be the Druid's muscle.
He has more than enough strength to take down a bull elk on his own.
No one eats before the pups.

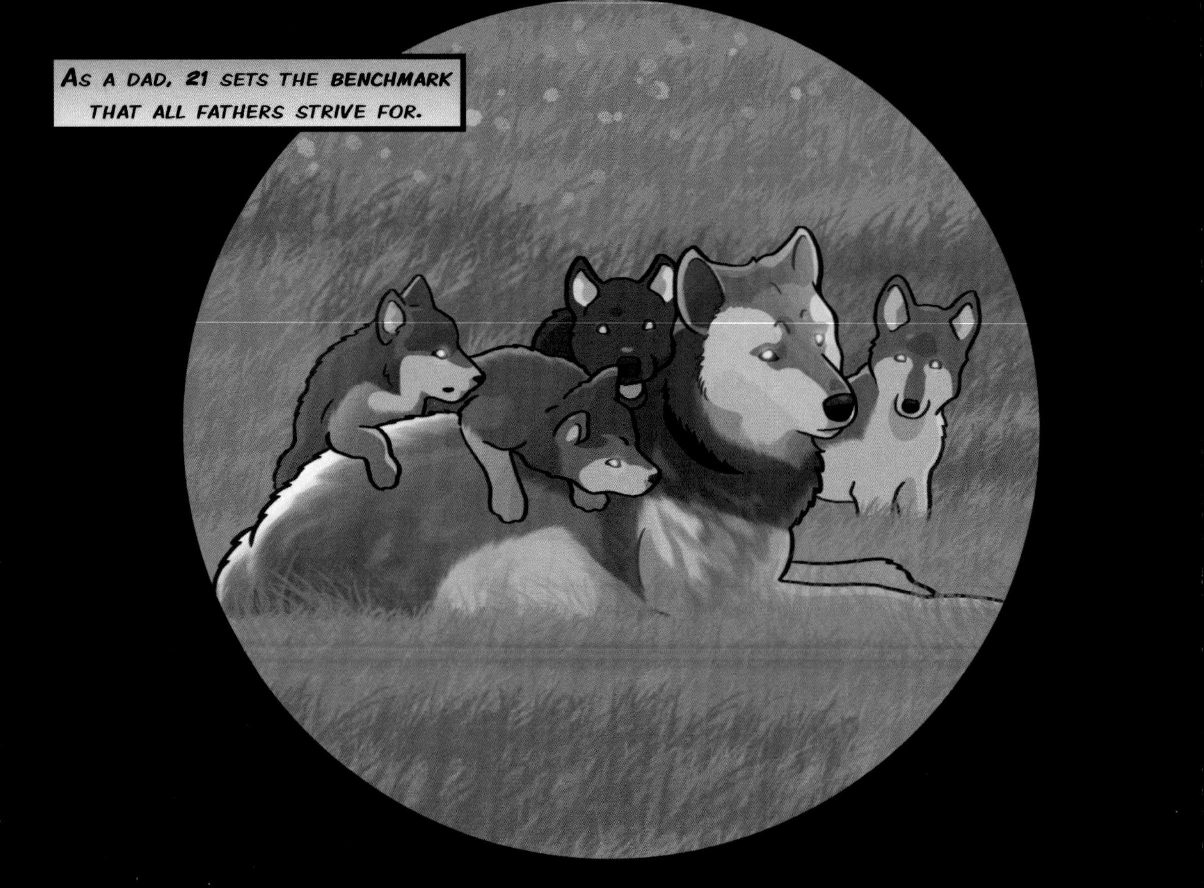
As a dad, 21 sets the benchmark that all fathers strive for.

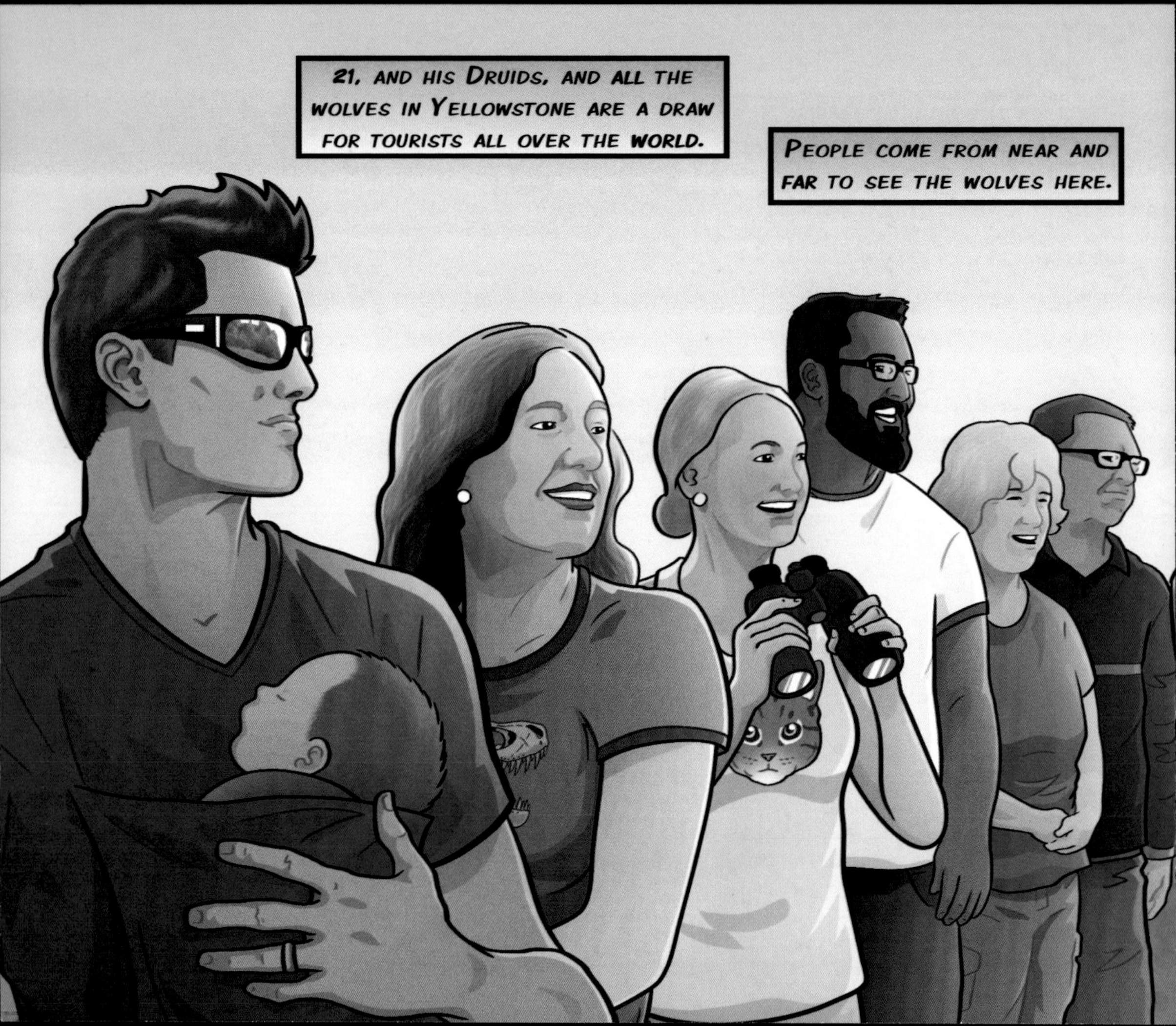
21, and his Druids, and all the wolves in Yellowstone are a draw for tourists all over the world.
People come from near and far to see the wolves here.

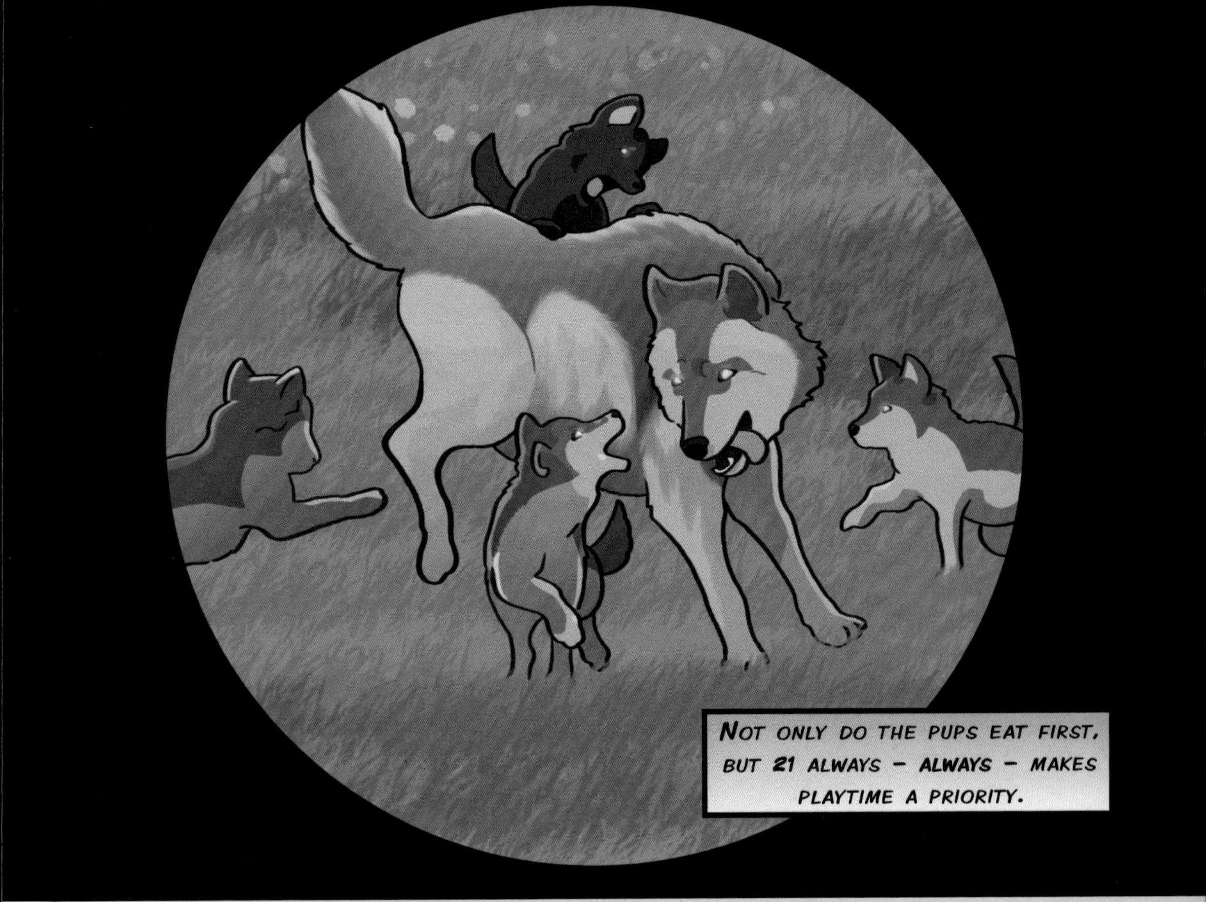
NOT ONLY DO THE PUPS EAT FIRST, BUT 21 ALWAYS – ALWAYS – MAKES PLAYTIME A PRIORITY.

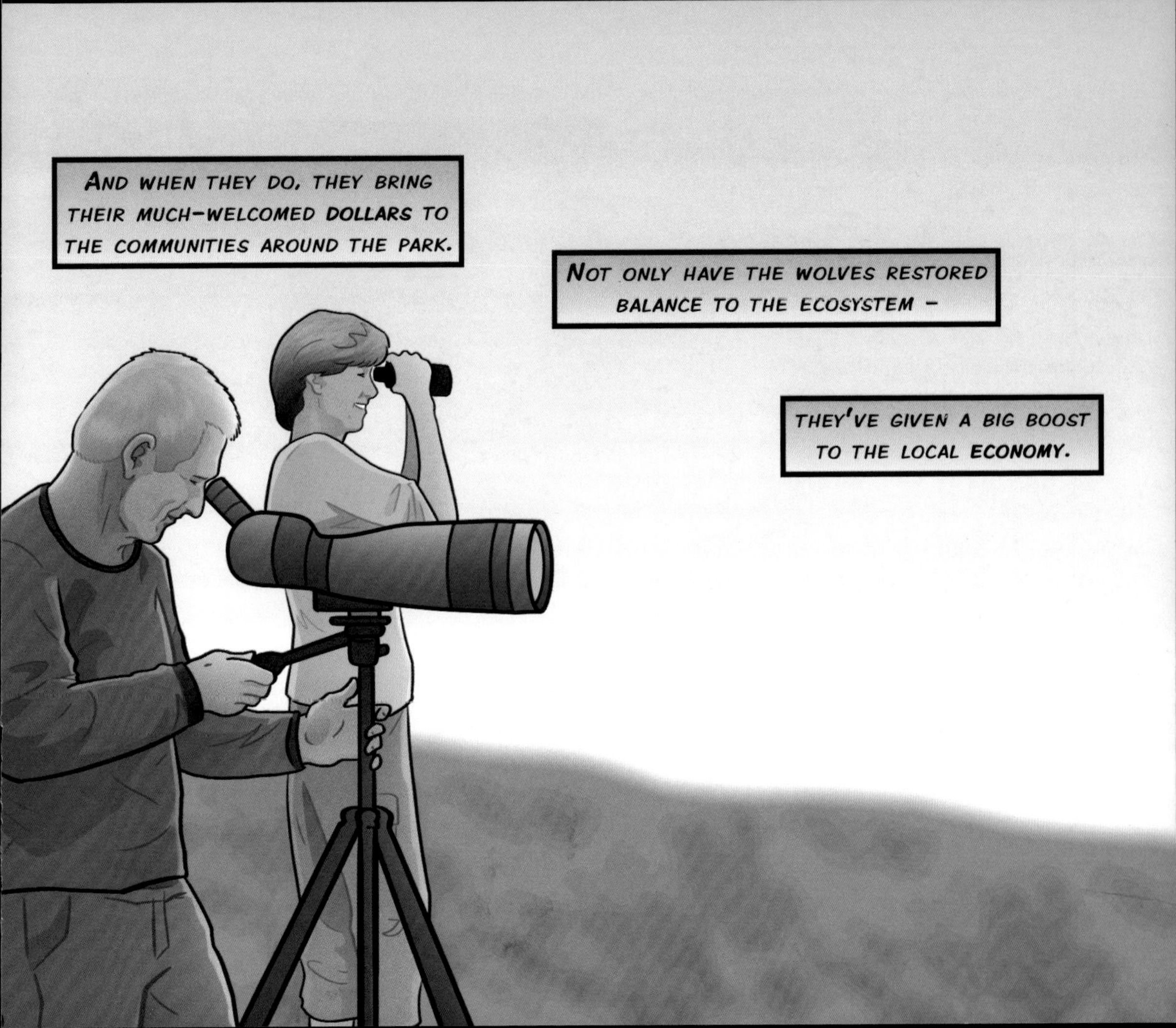
AND WHEN THEY DO, THEY BRING THEIR MUCH-WELCOMED DOLLARS TO THE COMMUNITIES AROUND THE PARK.
NOT ONLY HAVE THE WOLVES RESTORED BALANCE TO THE ECOSYSTEM –
THEY'VE GIVEN A BIG BOOST TO THE LOCAL ECONOMY.

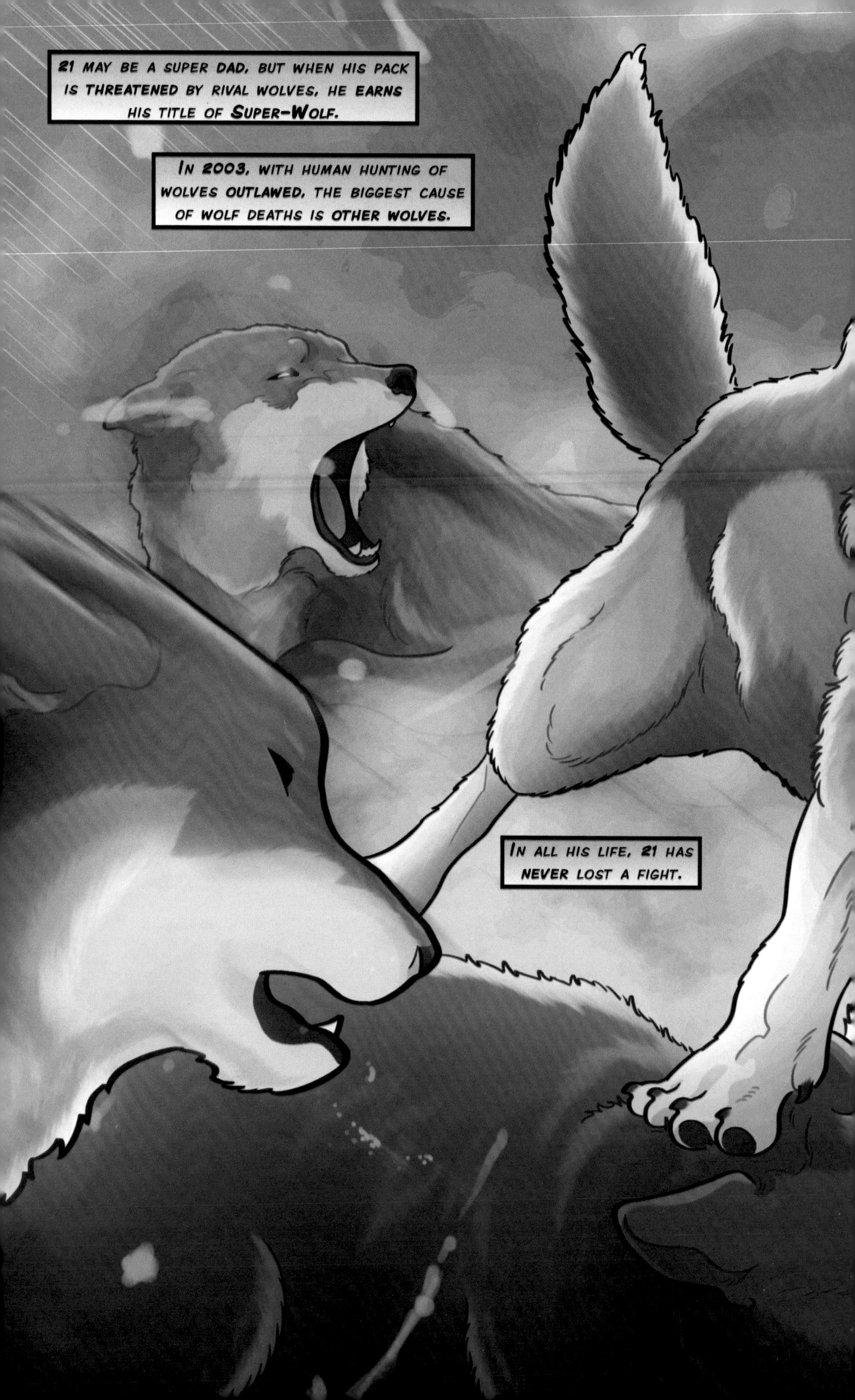

21 MAY BE A SUPER DAD, BUT WHEN HIS PACK IS THREATENED BY RIVAL WOLVES, HE EARNS HIS TITLE OF SUPER-WOLF.
IN 2003, WITH HUMAN HUNTING OF WOLVES OUTLAWED, THE BIGGEST CAUSE OF WOLF DEATHS IS OTHER WOLVES.
IN ALL HIS LIFE, 21 HAS NEVER LOST A FIGHT.

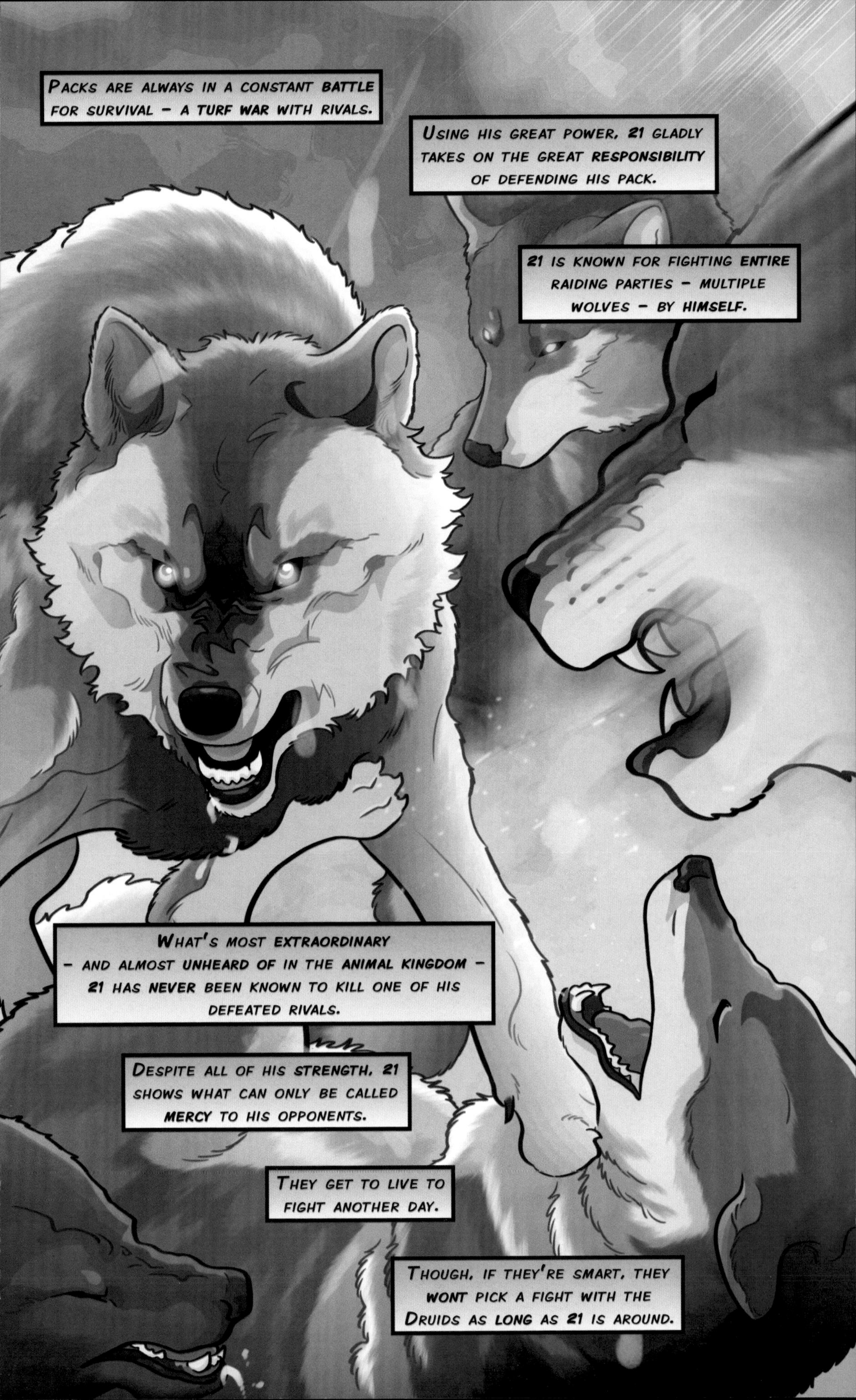
PACKS ARE ALWAYS IN A CONSTANT BATTLE FOR SURVIVAL - A TURF WAR WITH RIVALS.
USING HIS GREAT POWER, 21 GLADLY TAKES ON THE GREAT RESPONSIBILITY OF DEFENDING HIS PACK.
21 IS KNOWN FOR FIGHTING ENTIRE RAIDING PARTIES - MULTIPLE WOLVES - BY HIMSELF.
WHAT'S MOST EXTRAORDINARY - AND ALMOST UNHEARD OF IN THE ANIMAL KINGDOM - 21 HAS NEVER BEEN KNOWN TO KILL ONE OF HIS DEFEATED RIVALS.
DESPITE ALL OF HIS STRENGTH, 21 SHOWS WHAT CAN ONLY BE CALLED MERCY TO HIS OPPONENTS.
THEY GET TO LIVE TO FIGHT ANOTHER DAY.
THOUGH, IF THEY'RE SMART, THEY WONT PICK A FIGHT WITH THE DRUIDS AS LONG AS 21 IS AROUND.

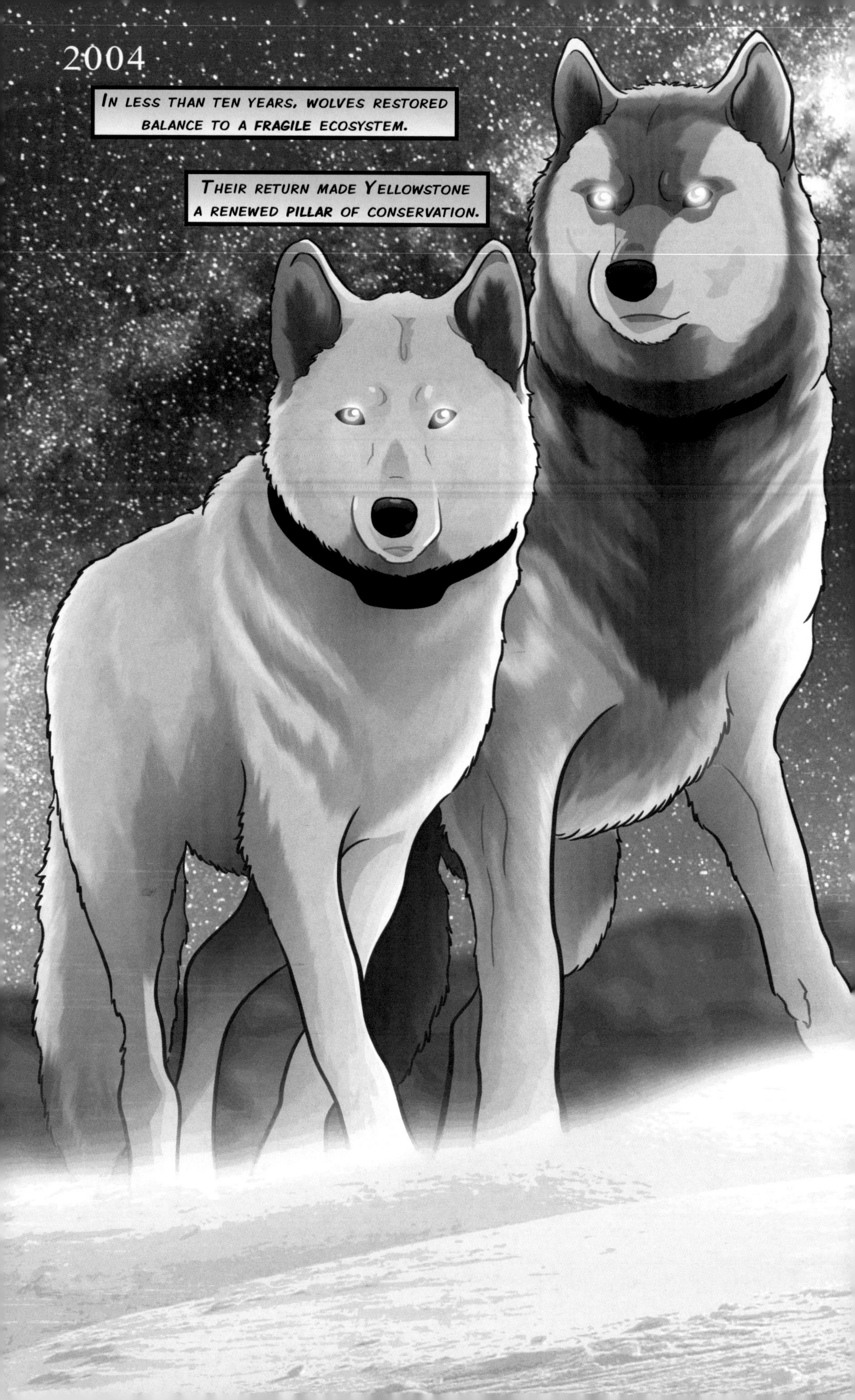
2004
In less than ten years, wolves restored balance to a fragile ecosystem.
Their return made Yellowstone a renewed pillar of conservation.

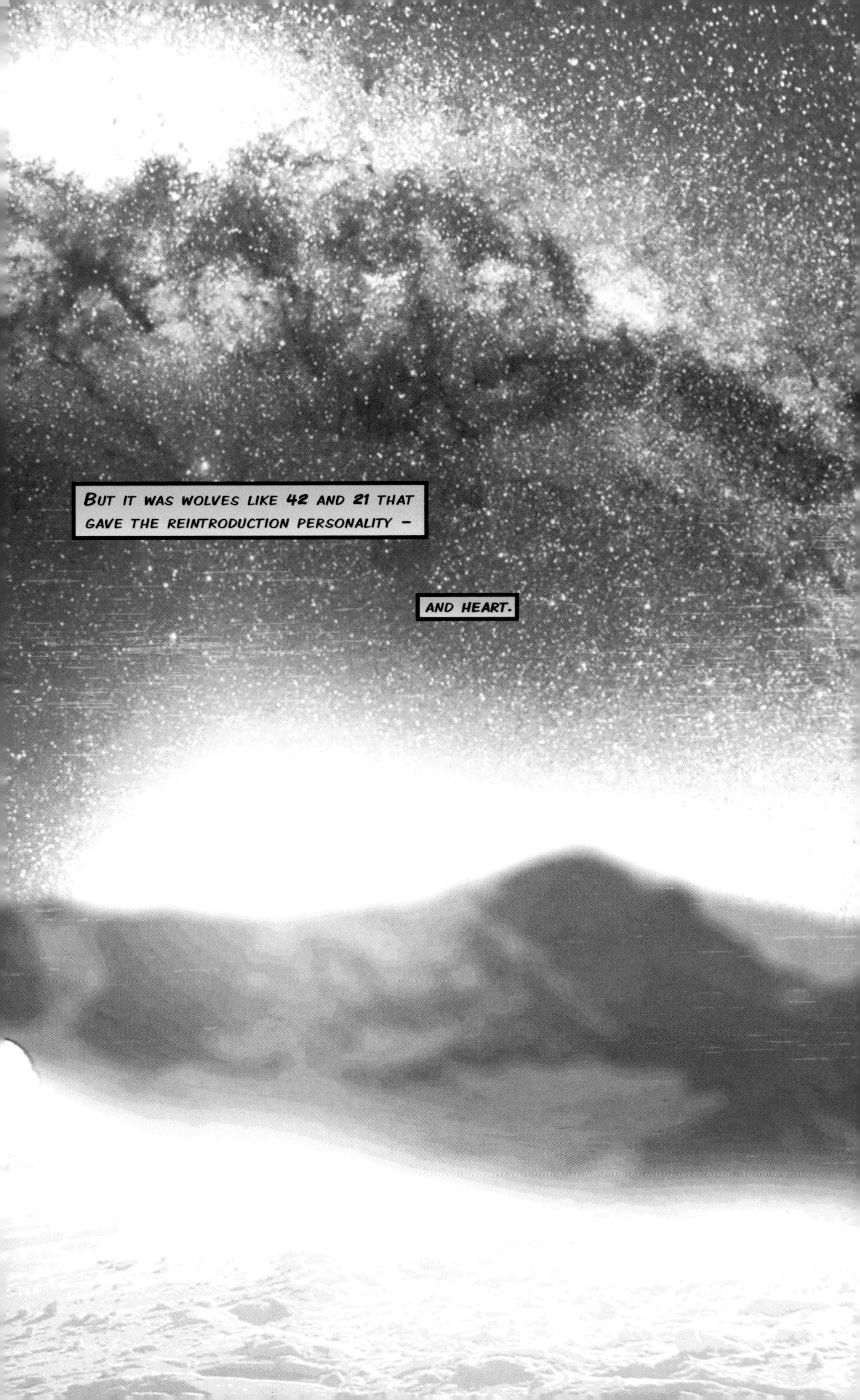
But it was wolves like 42 and 21 that gave the reintroduction personality –
and heart.

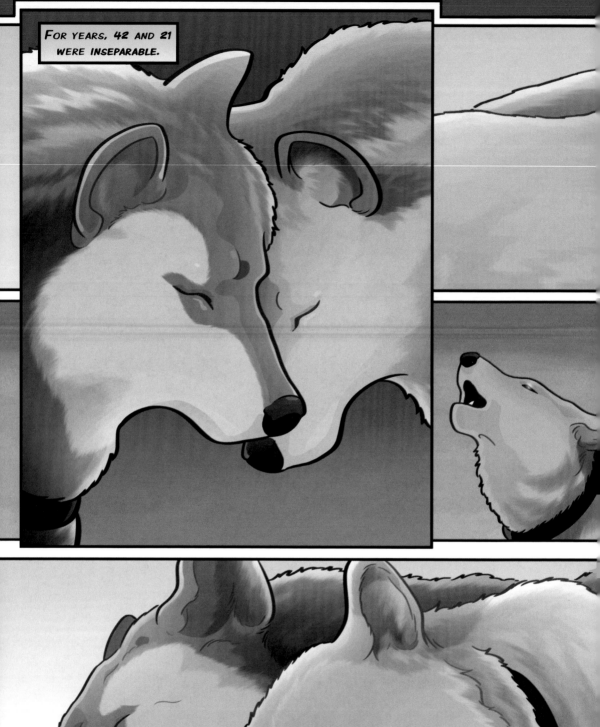

FOR YEARS, 42 AND 21 WERE INSEPARABLE.

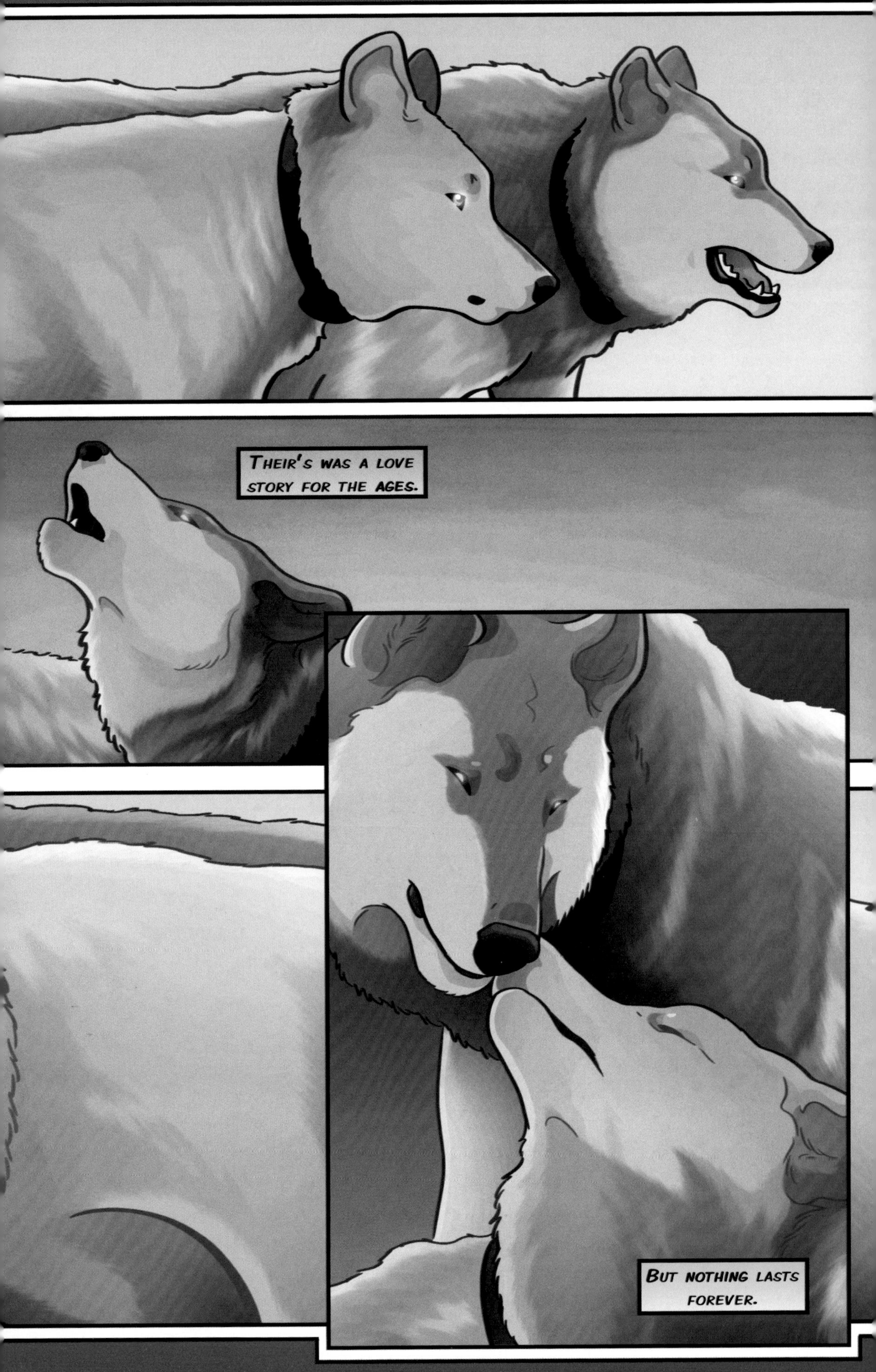
THEIR'S WAS A LOVE STORY FOR THE AGES.
BUT NOTHING LASTS FOREVER.

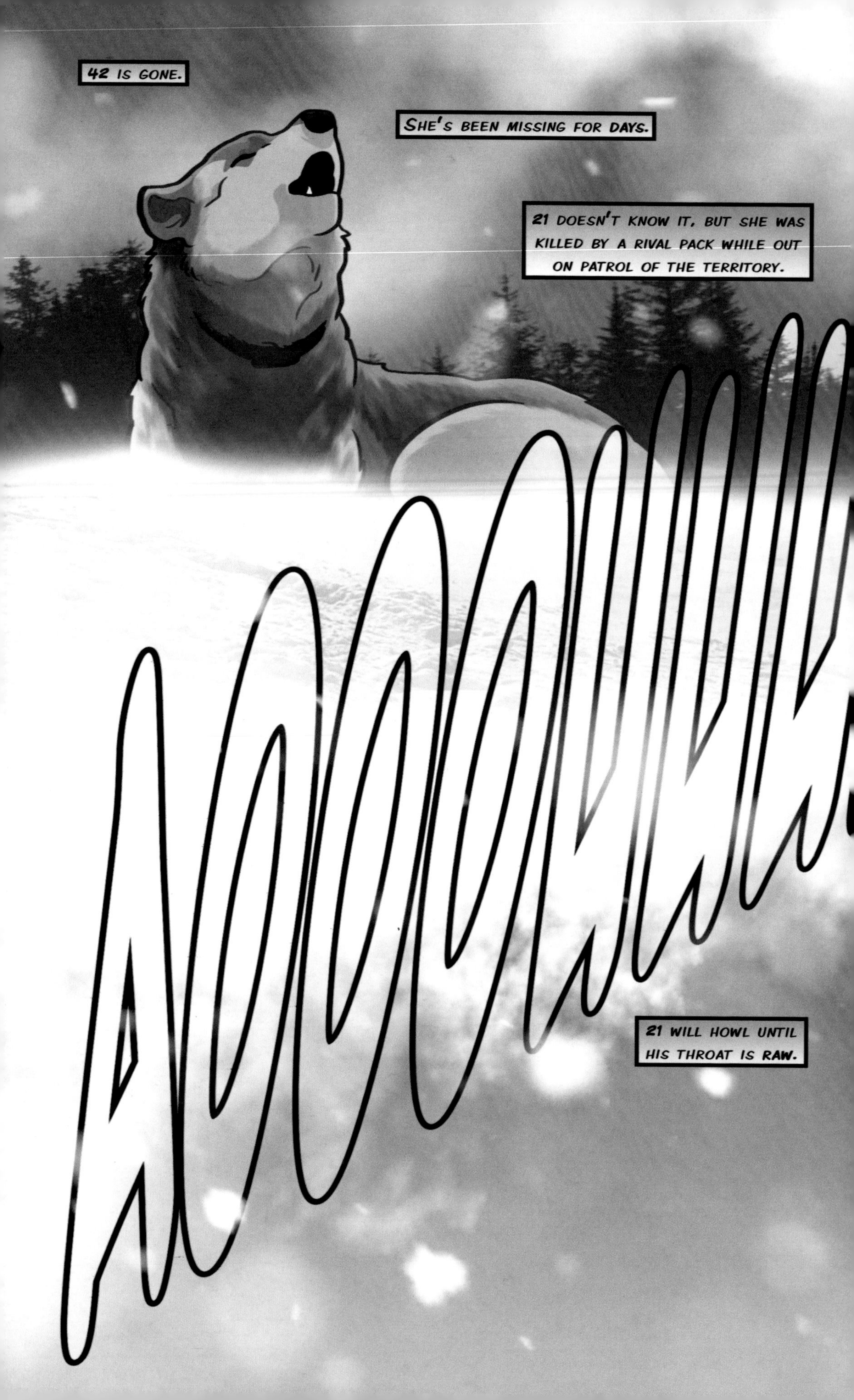

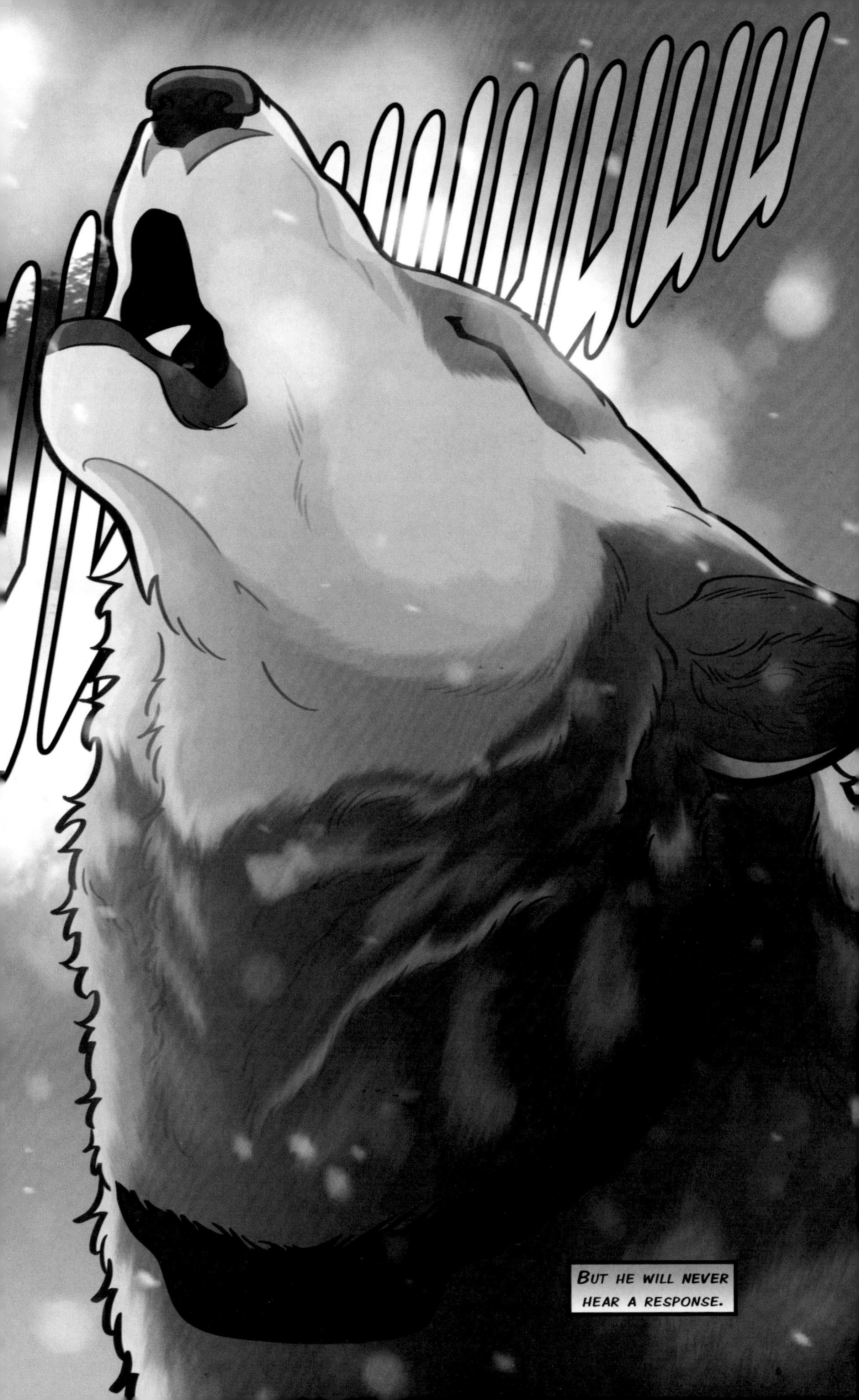
But he will never hear a response.

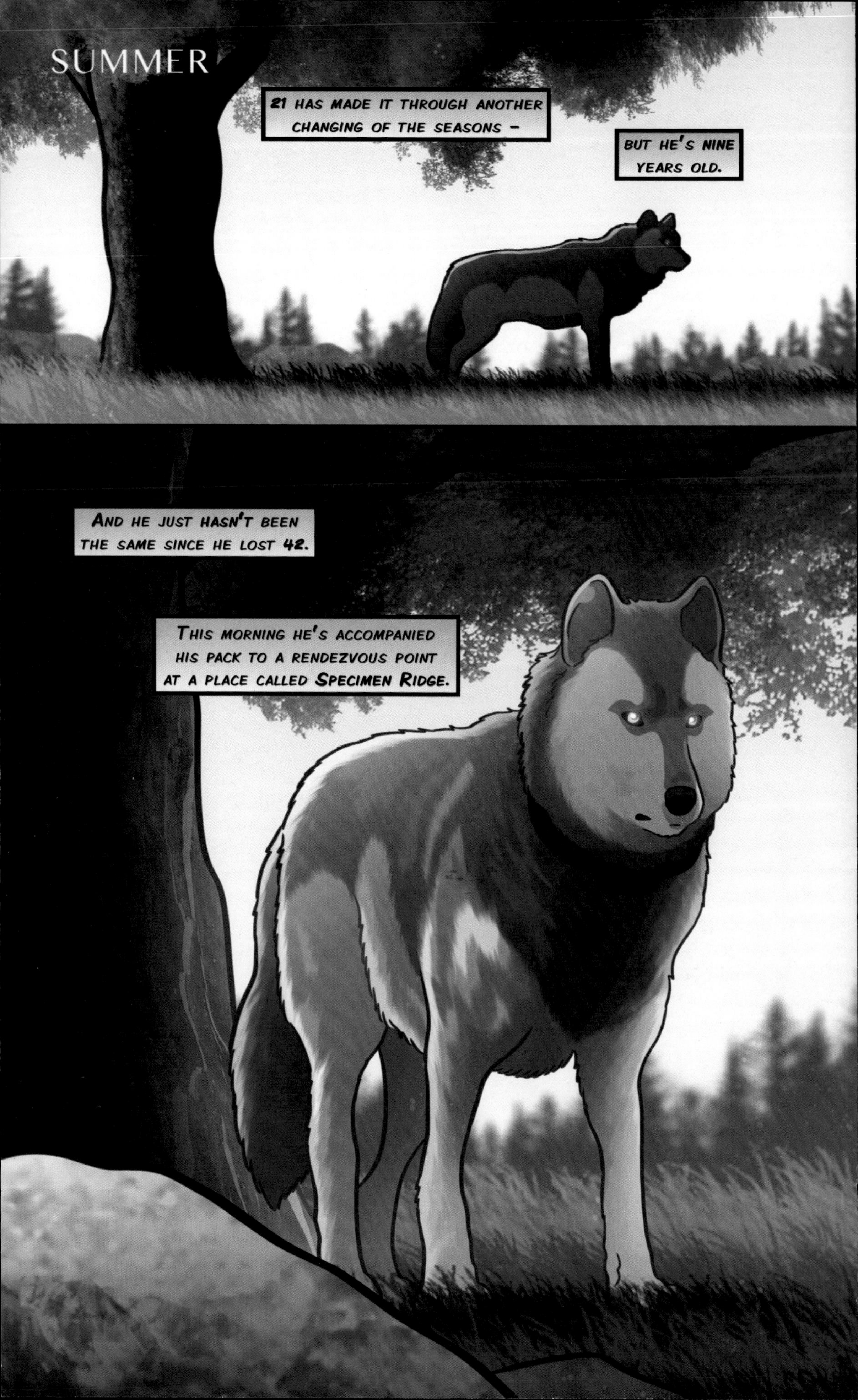
SUMMER
21 HAS MADE IT THROUGH ANOTHER CHANGING OF THE SEASONS –
BUT HE'S NINE YEARS OLD.
AND HE JUST HASN'T BEEN THE SAME SINCE HE LOST 42.
THIS MORNING HE'S ACCOMPANIED HIS PACK TO A RENDEZVOUS POINT AT A PLACE CALLED SPECIMEN RIDGE.

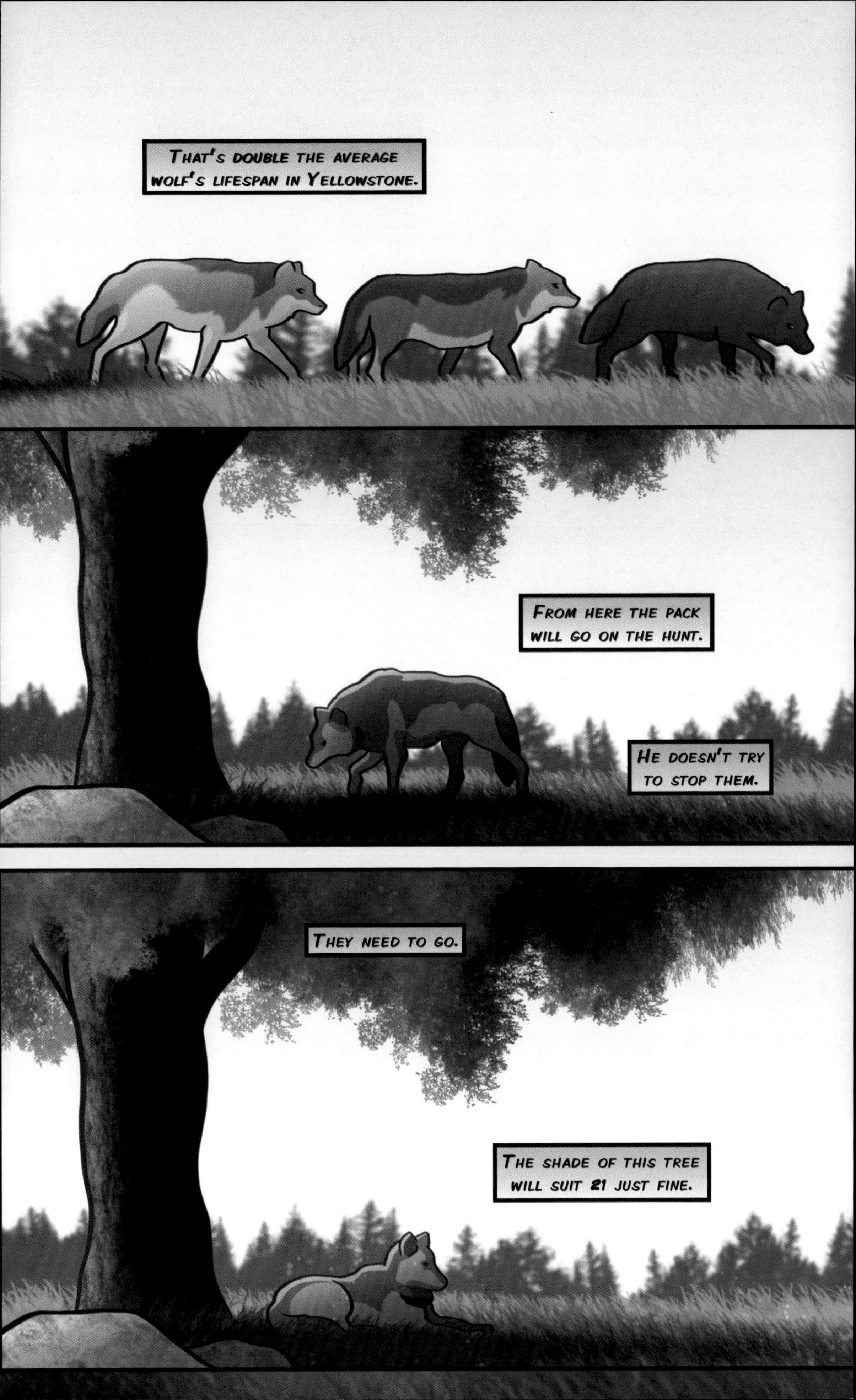

That's double the average wolf's lifespan in Yellowstone.
From here the pack will go on the hunt.
He doesn't try to stop them.
They need to go.
The shade of this tree will suit 21 just fine.

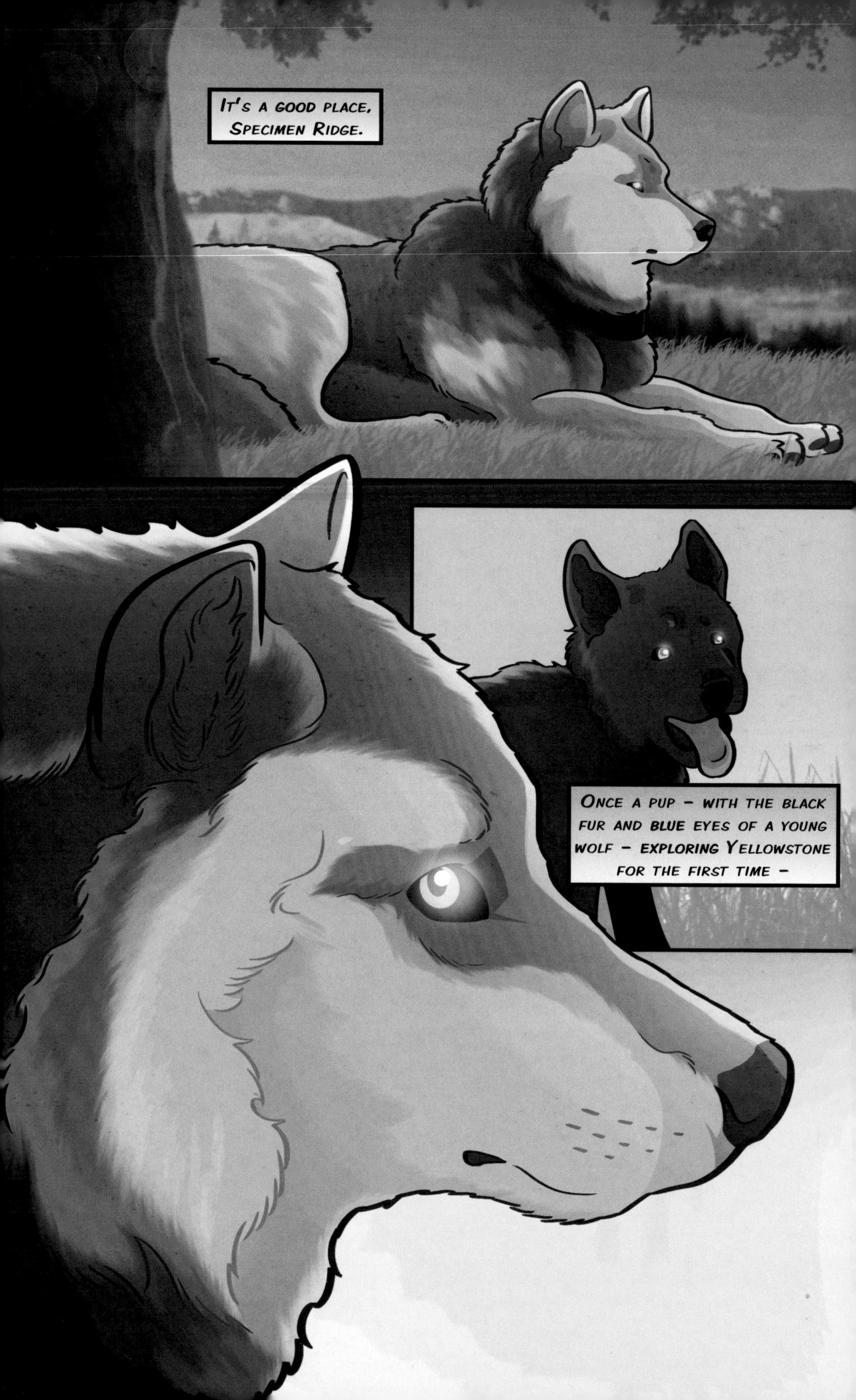
It's a good place, Specimen Ridge.
Once a pup – with the black fur and blue eyes of a young wolf – exploring Yellowstone for the first time –

21 HAS SPENT THE WHOLE DAY LOOKING OUT OVER HIS HOME.

GROWING INTO A POWERFUL PACK MEMBER—

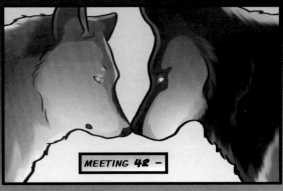

MEETING 42 –

AND BECOMING A LEADER –

ONE WHO WAS STRONG –

BUT NEVER CRUEL.

IT'S BEEN A LONG LIFE FOR A WOLF.

AND A GOOD ONE.

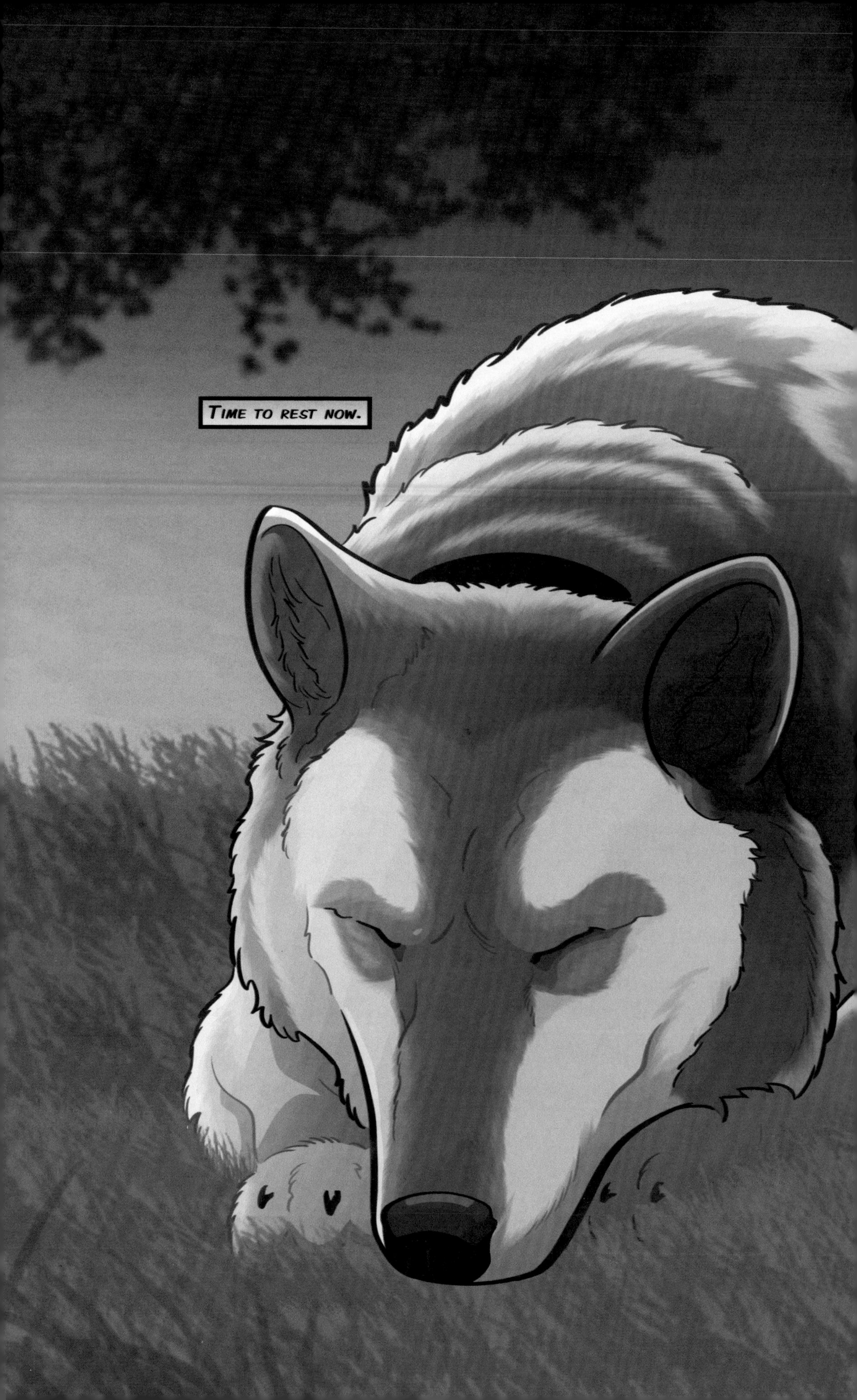
TIME TO REST NOW.

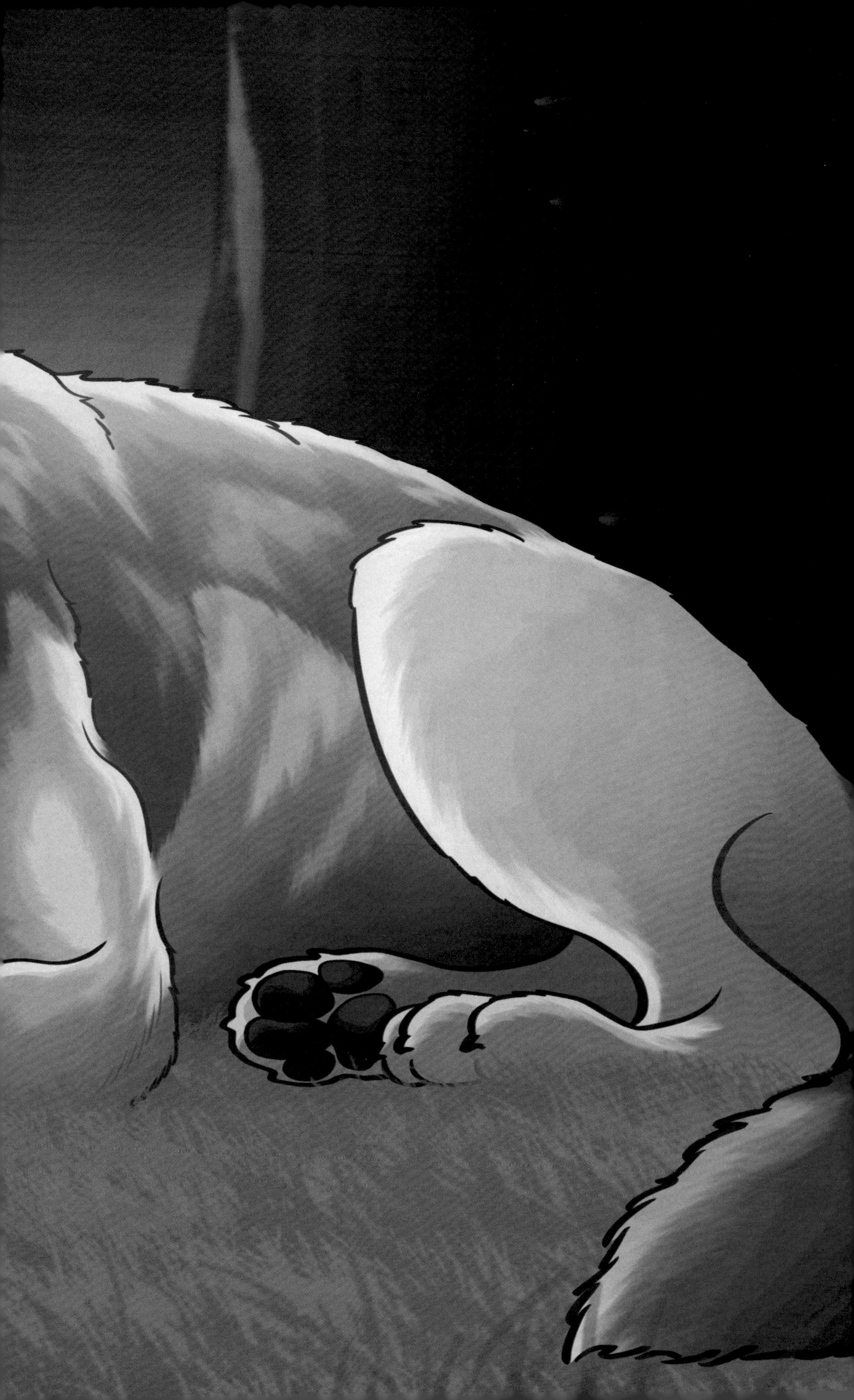

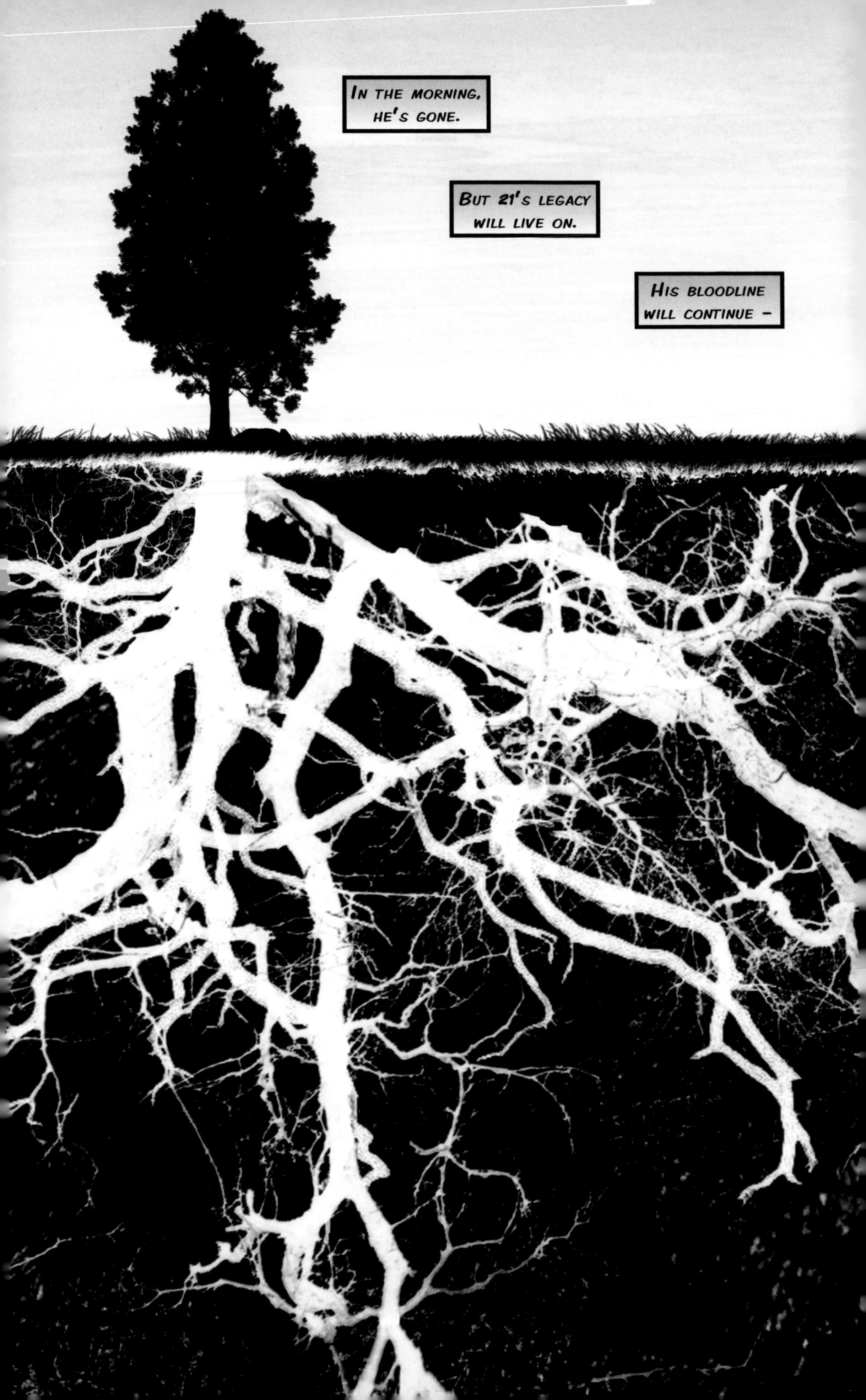
In the morning, he's gone.
But 21's legacy will live on.
His bloodline will continue –

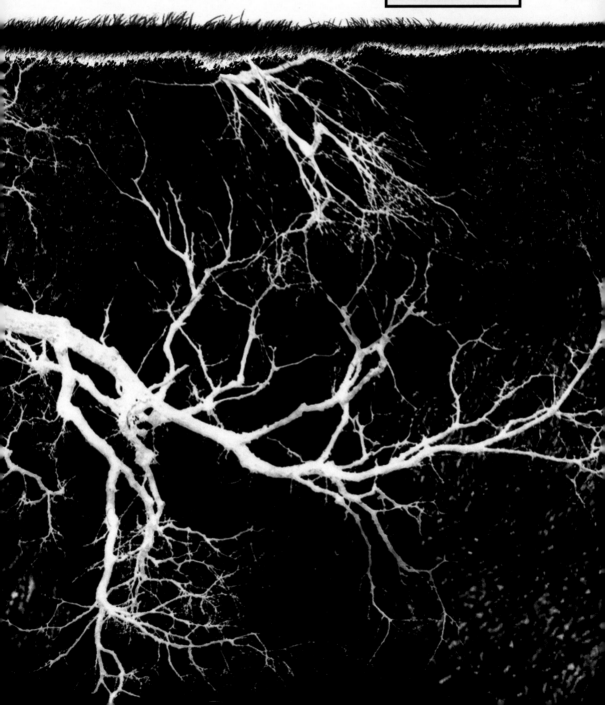

BEYOND THE DRUID PEAK PACK —

AND BECOME THE VERY BEATING HEART OF YELLOWSTONE.

THE BIG BAD WOLF

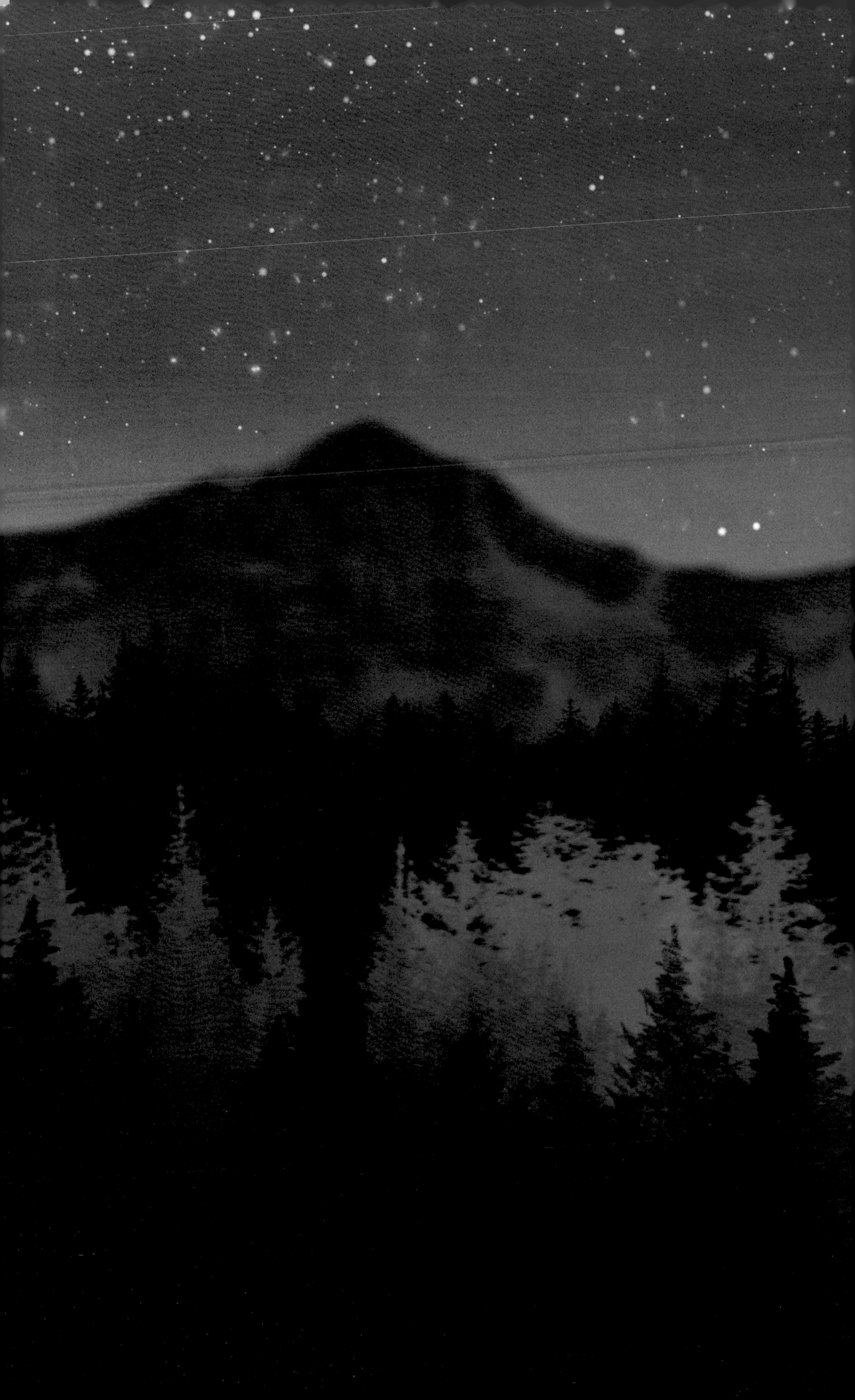

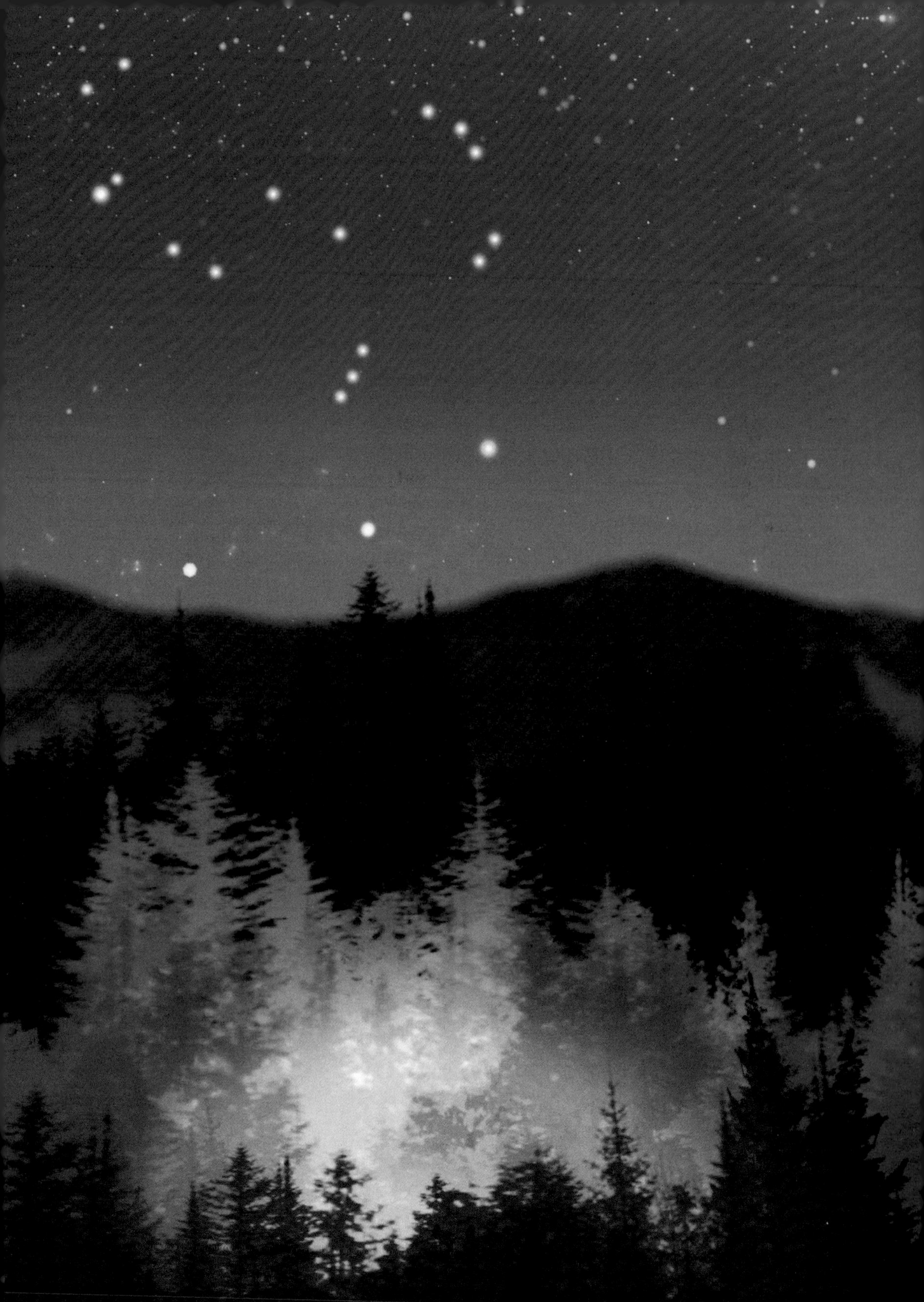

THE ICE AGE

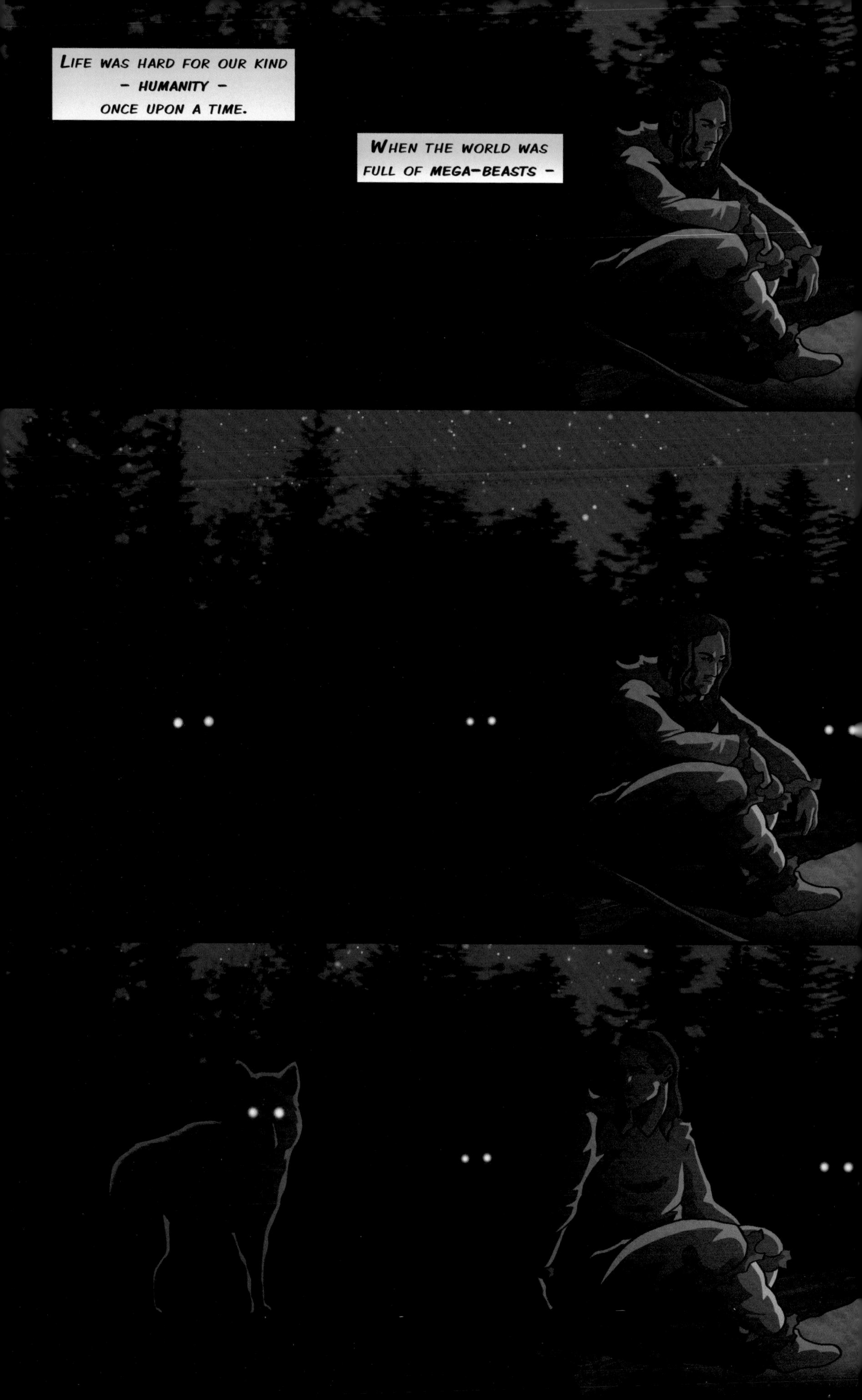
LIFE WAS HARD FOR OUR KIND
- HUMANITY -
ONCE UPON A TIME.
WHEN THE WORLD WAS FULL OF MEGA-BEASTS -

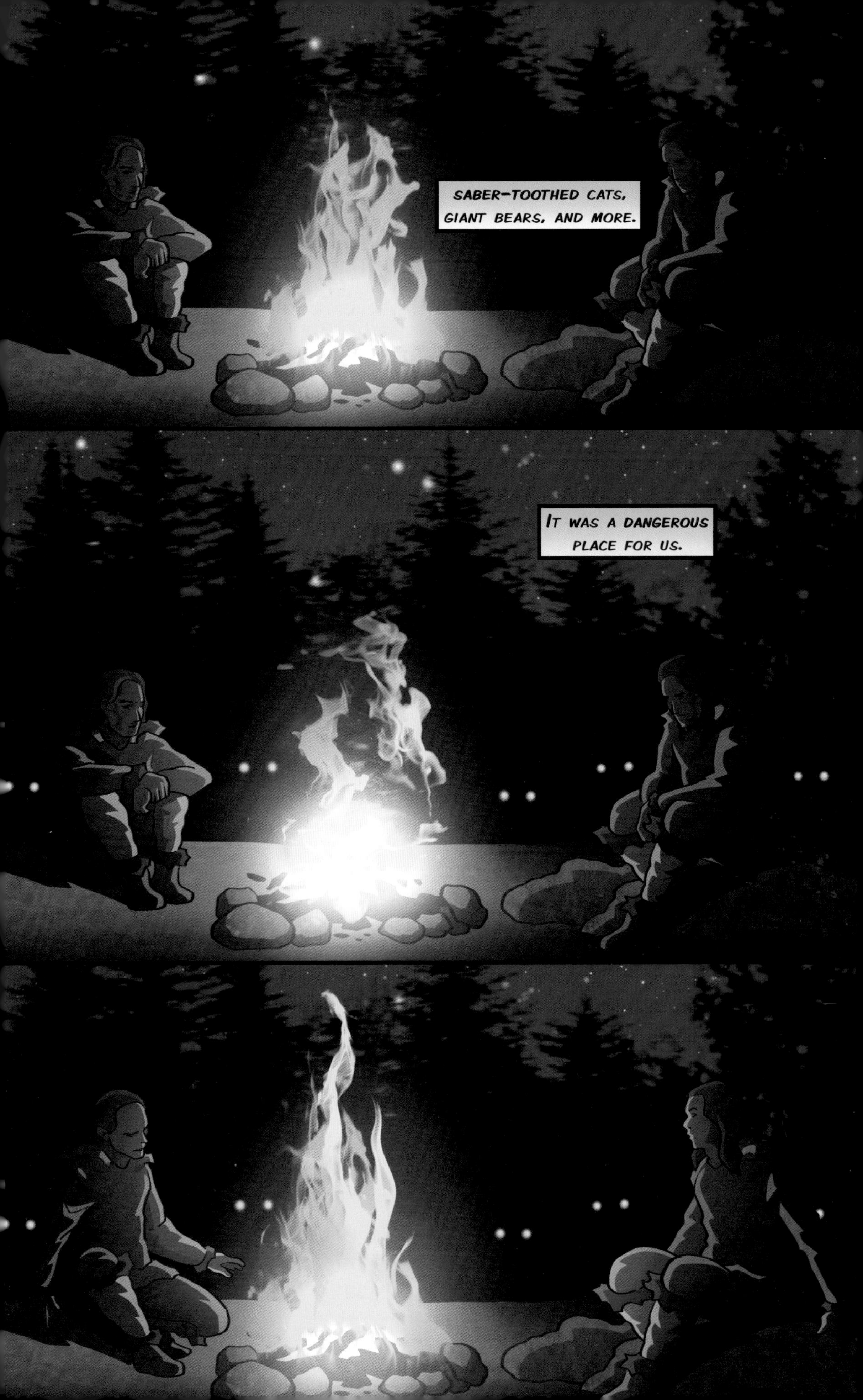
SABER-TOOTHED CATS, GIANT BEARS, AND MORE.
IT WAS A DANGEROUS PLACE FOR US.

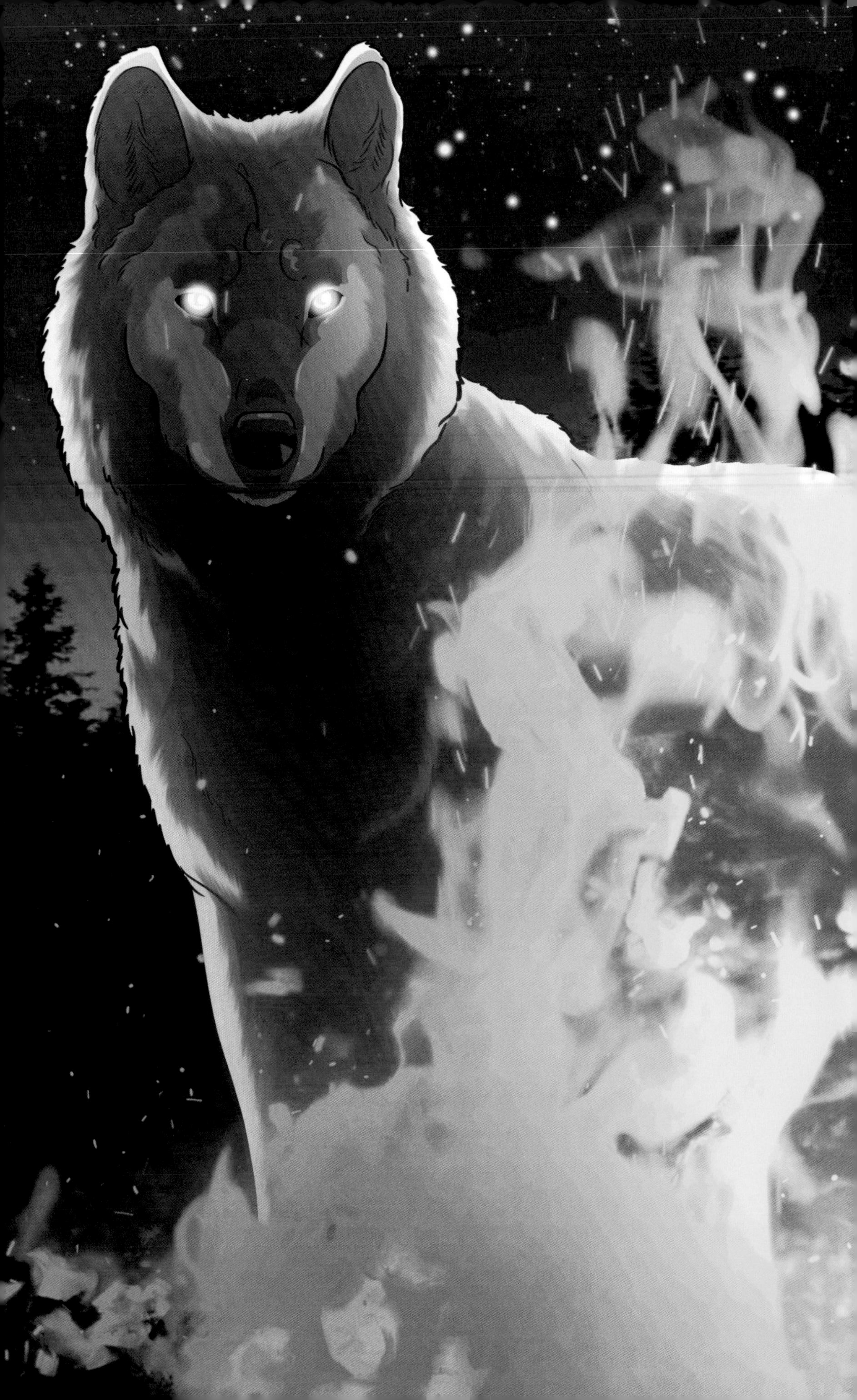

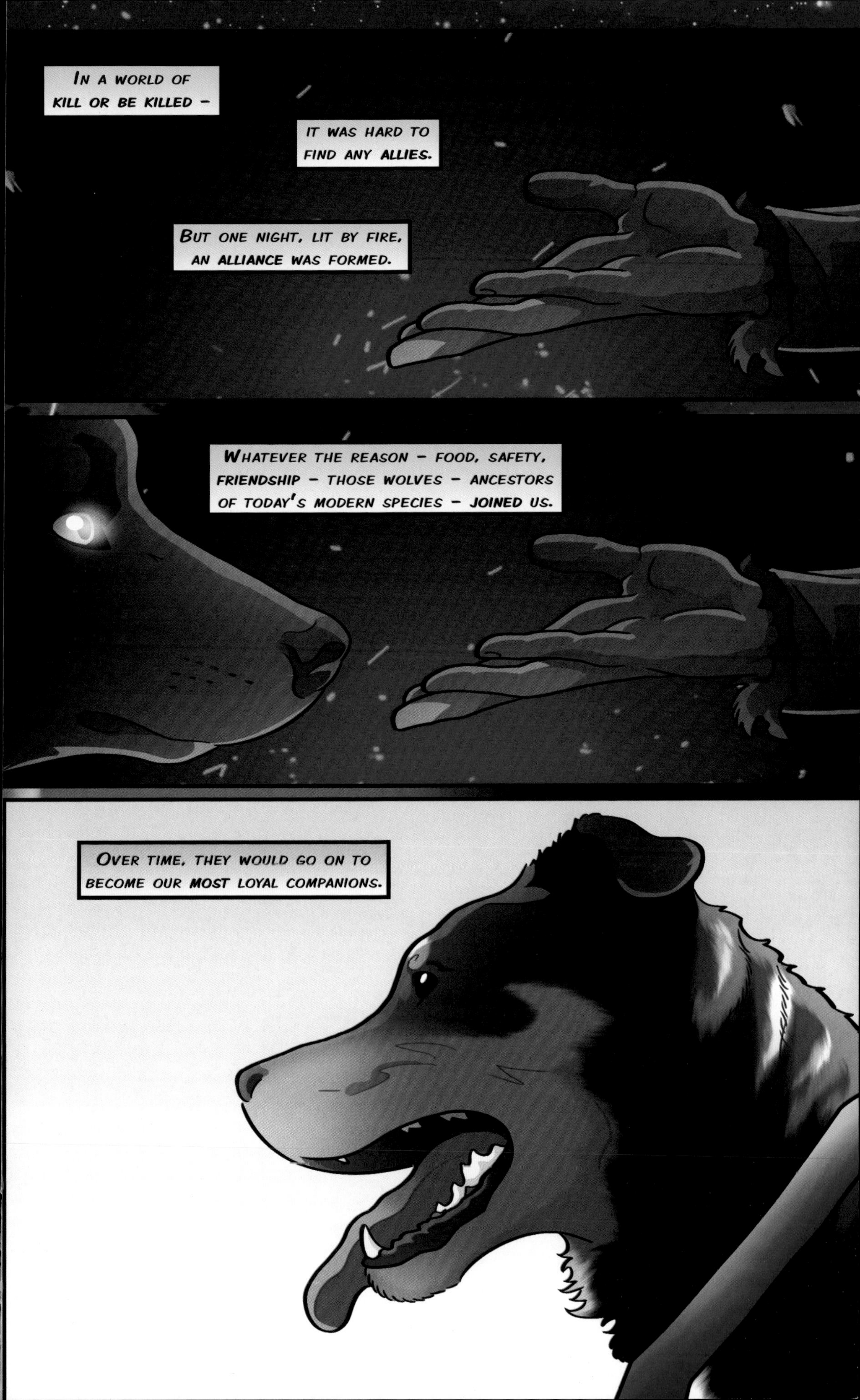
In a world of kill or be killed –
it was hard to find any allies.
But one night, lit by fire, an alliance was formed.
Whatever the reason – food, safety, friendship – those wolves – ancestors of today's modern species – joined us.
Over time, they would go on to become our most loyal companions.

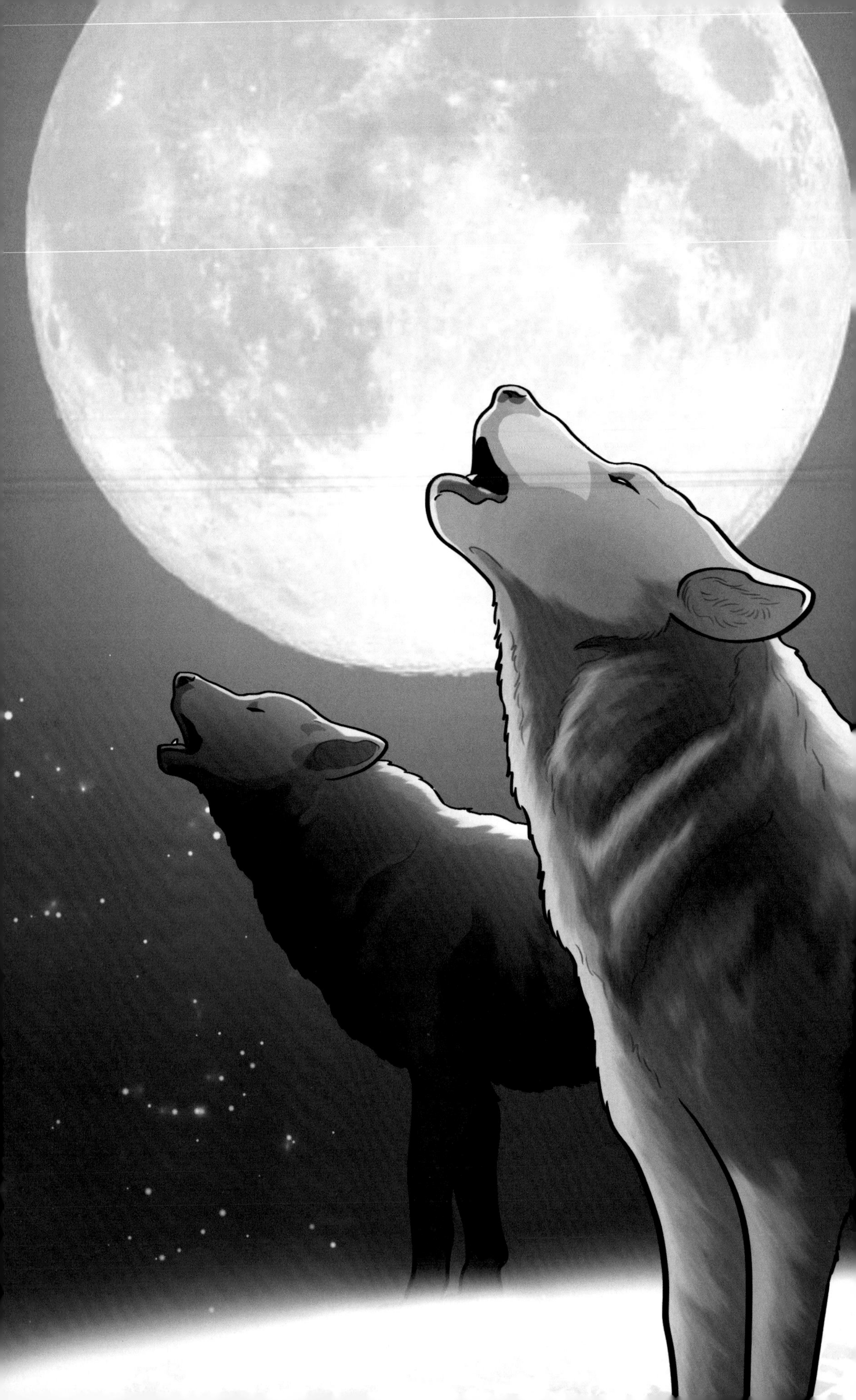

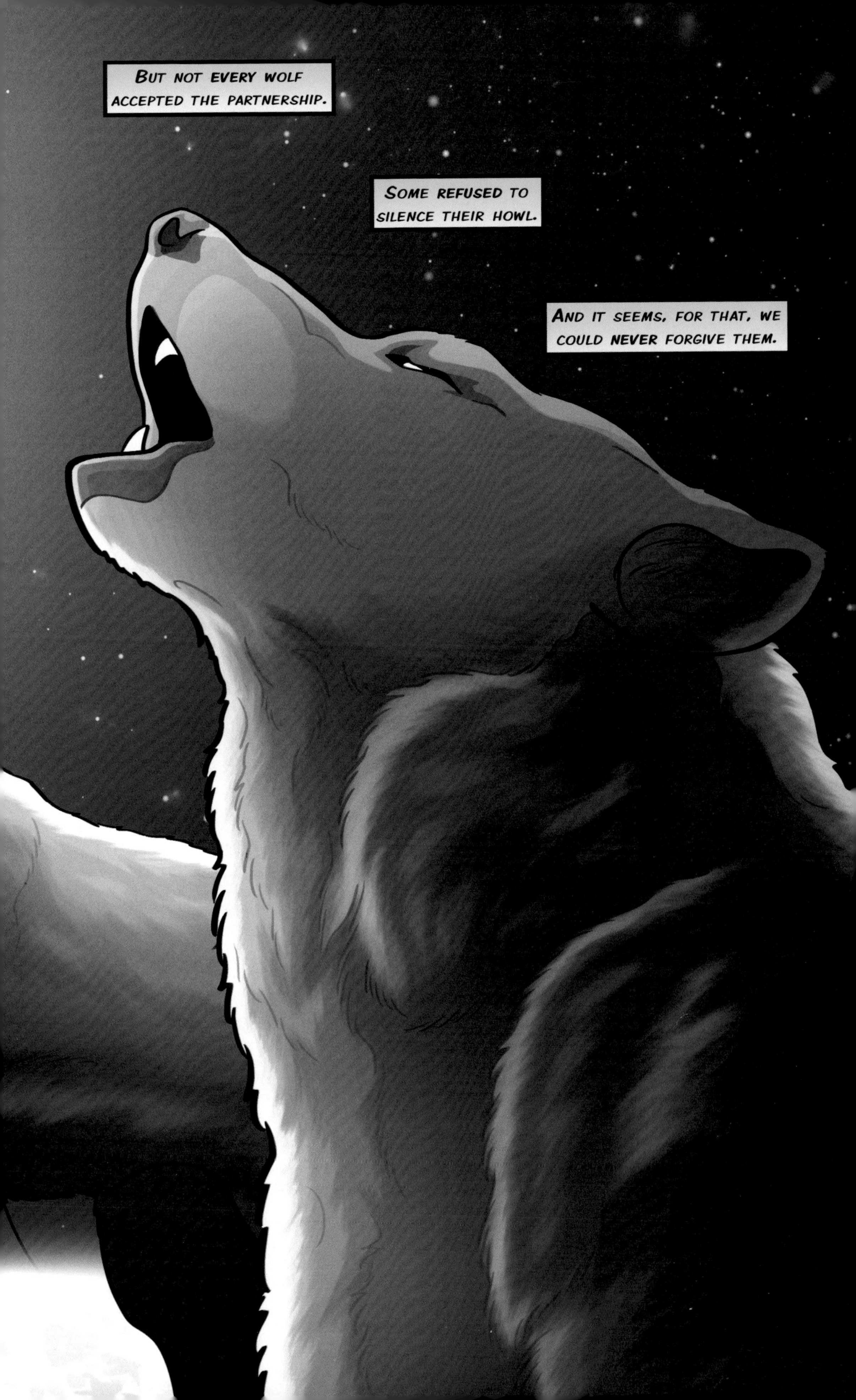
BUT NOT EVERY WOLF ACCEPTED THE PARTNERSHIP.
SOME REFUSED TO SILENCE THEIR HOWL.
AND IT SEEMS, FOR THAT, WE COULD NEVER FORGIVE THEM.

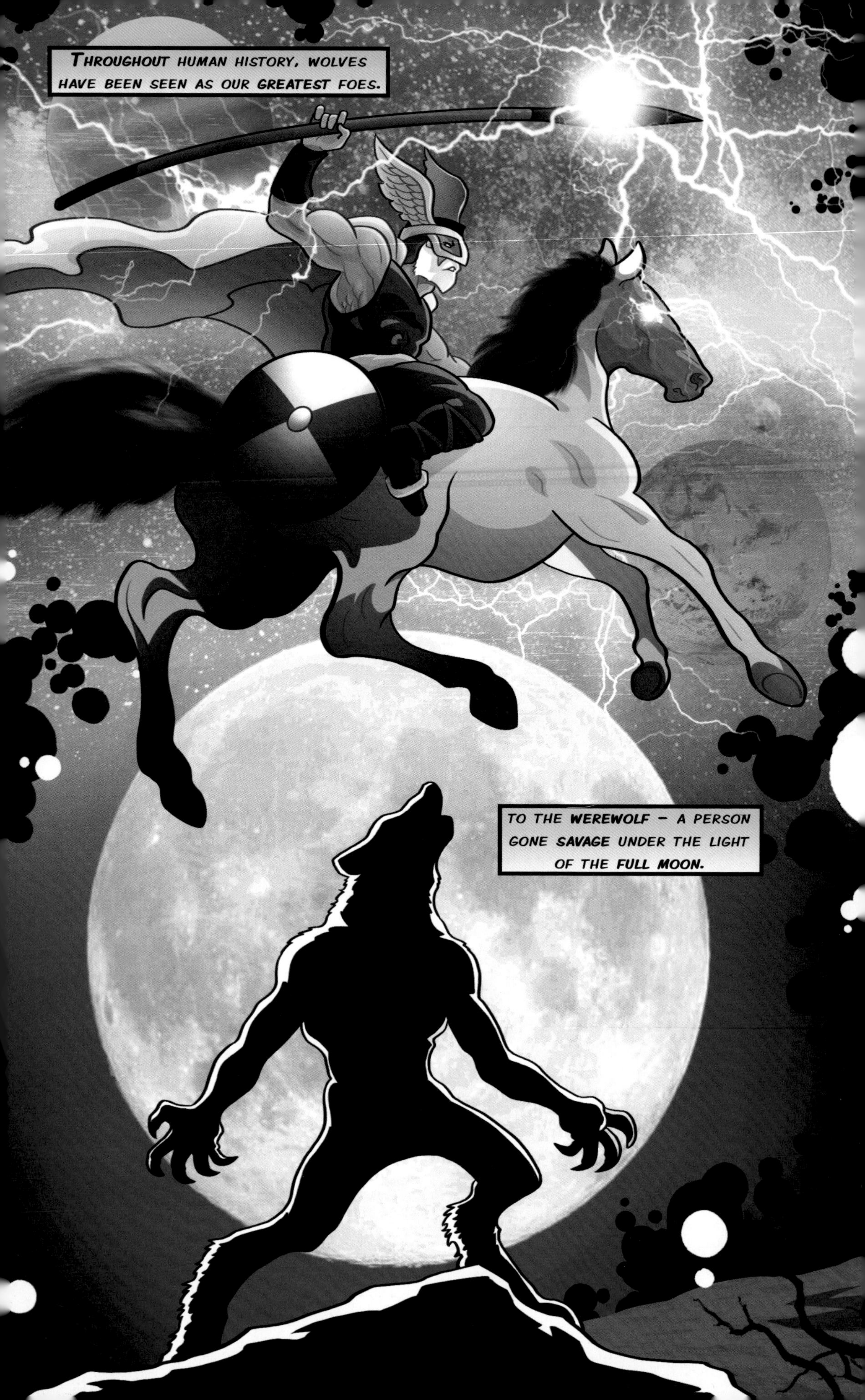
THROUGHOUT HUMAN HISTORY, WOLVES HAVE BEEN SEEN AS OUR GREATEST FOES.
TO THE WEREWOLF – A PERSON GONE SAVAGE UNDER THE LIGHT OF THE FULL MOON.

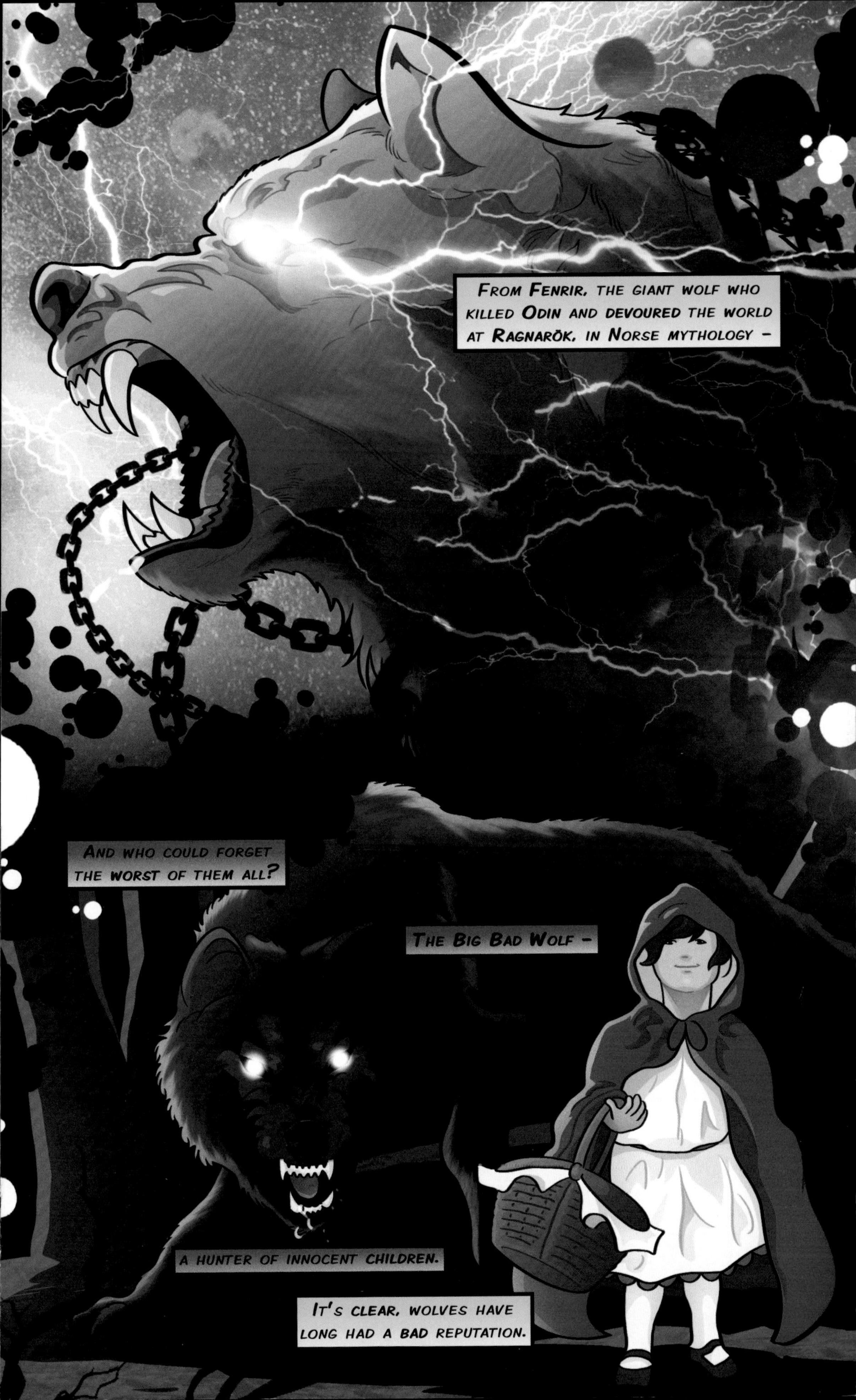
FROM FENRIR, THE GIANT WOLF WHO KILLED ODIN AND DEVOURED THE WORLD AT RAGNARÖK, IN NORSE MYTHOLOGY –
AND WHO COULD FORGET THE WORST OF THEM ALL?
THE BIG BAD WOLF –
A HUNTER OF INNOCENT CHILDREN.
IT'S CLEAR, WOLVES HAVE LONG HAD A BAD REPUTATION.

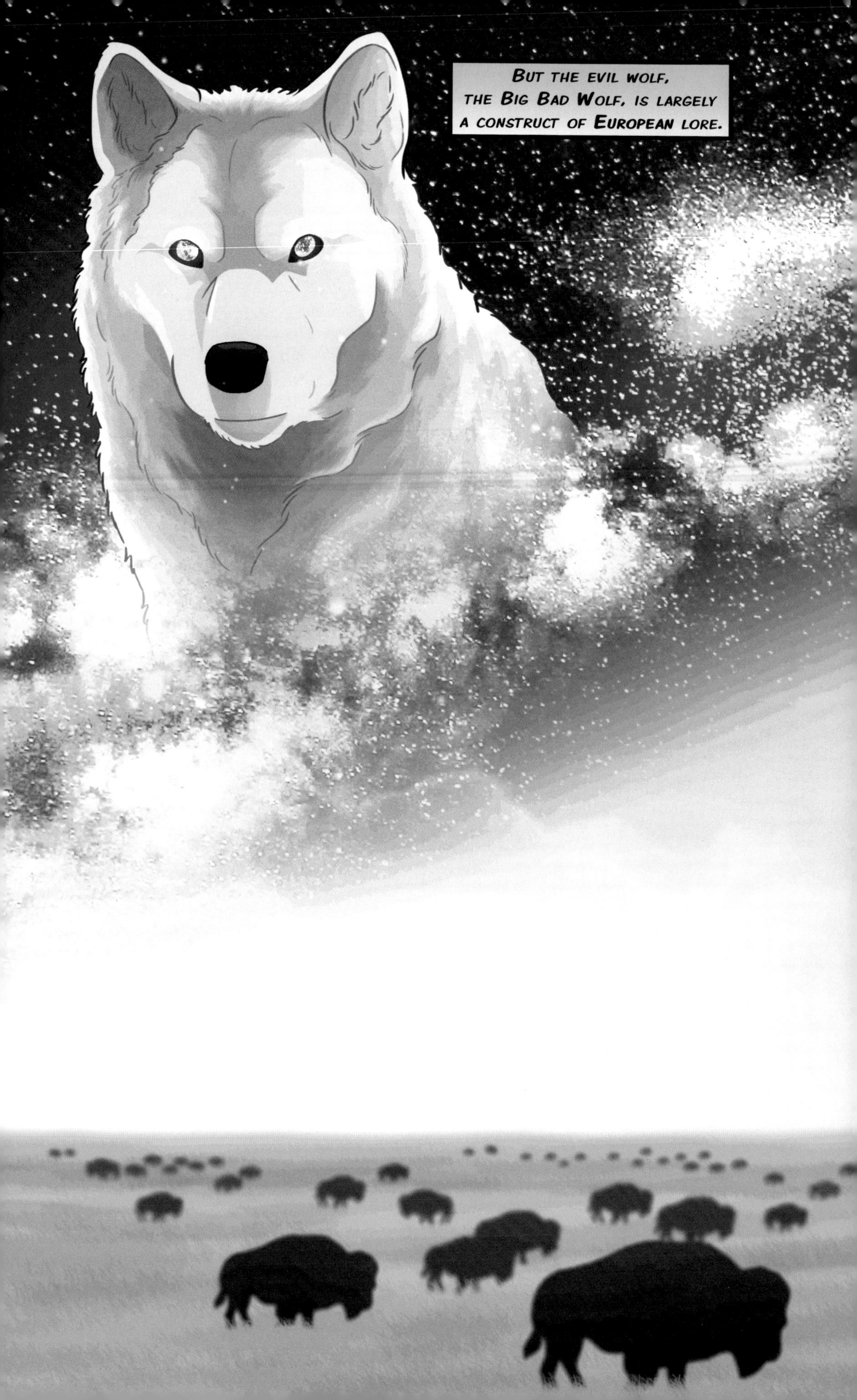
BUT THE EVIL WOLF, THE BIG BAD WOLF, IS LARGELY A CONSTRUCT OF EUROPEAN LORE.

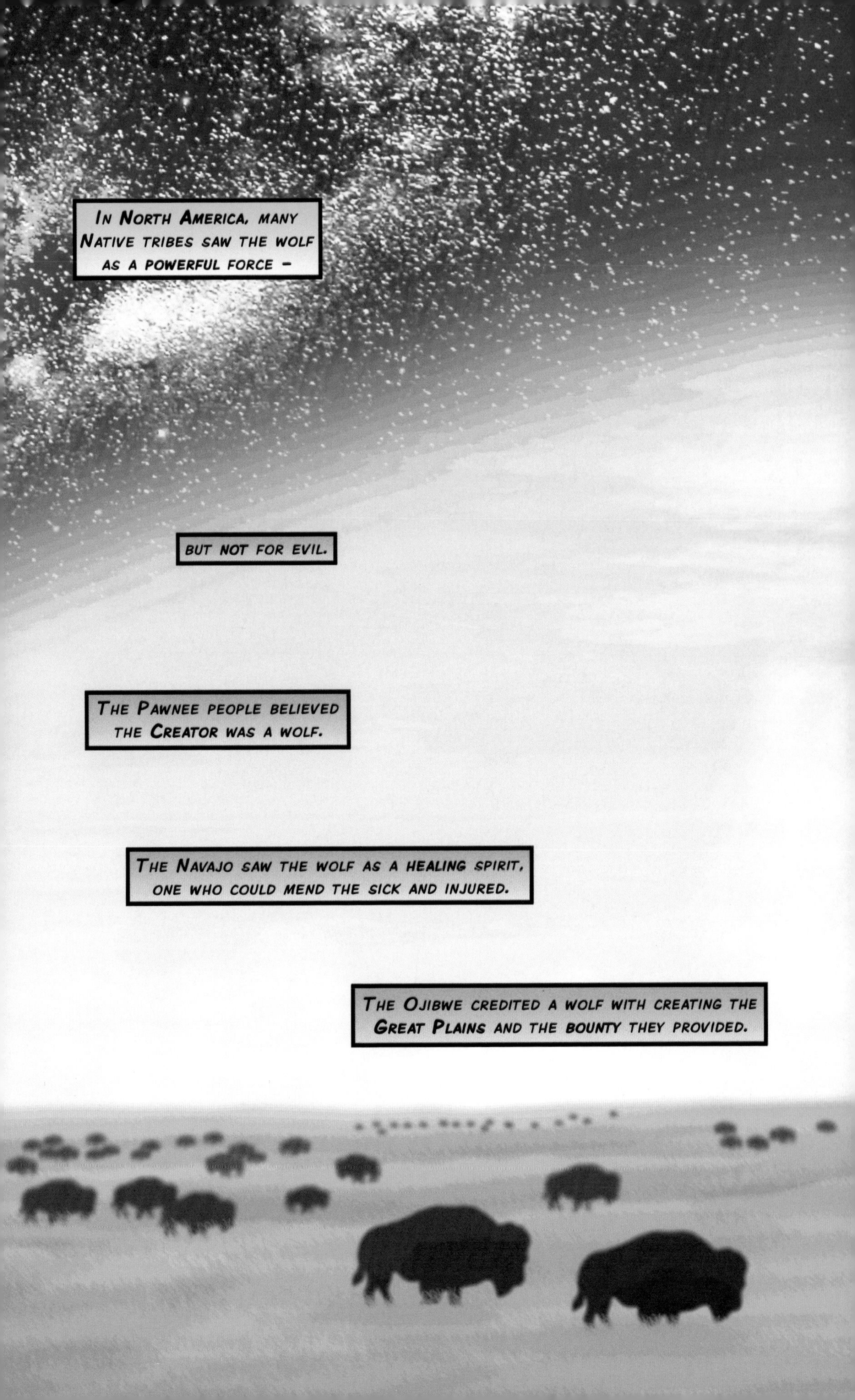

In North America, many Native tribes saw the wolf as a powerful force –
but not for evil.
The Pawnee people believed the Creator was a wolf.
The Navajo saw the wolf as a healing spirit, one who could mend the sick and injured.
The Ojibwe credited a wolf with creating the Great Plains and the bounty they provided.

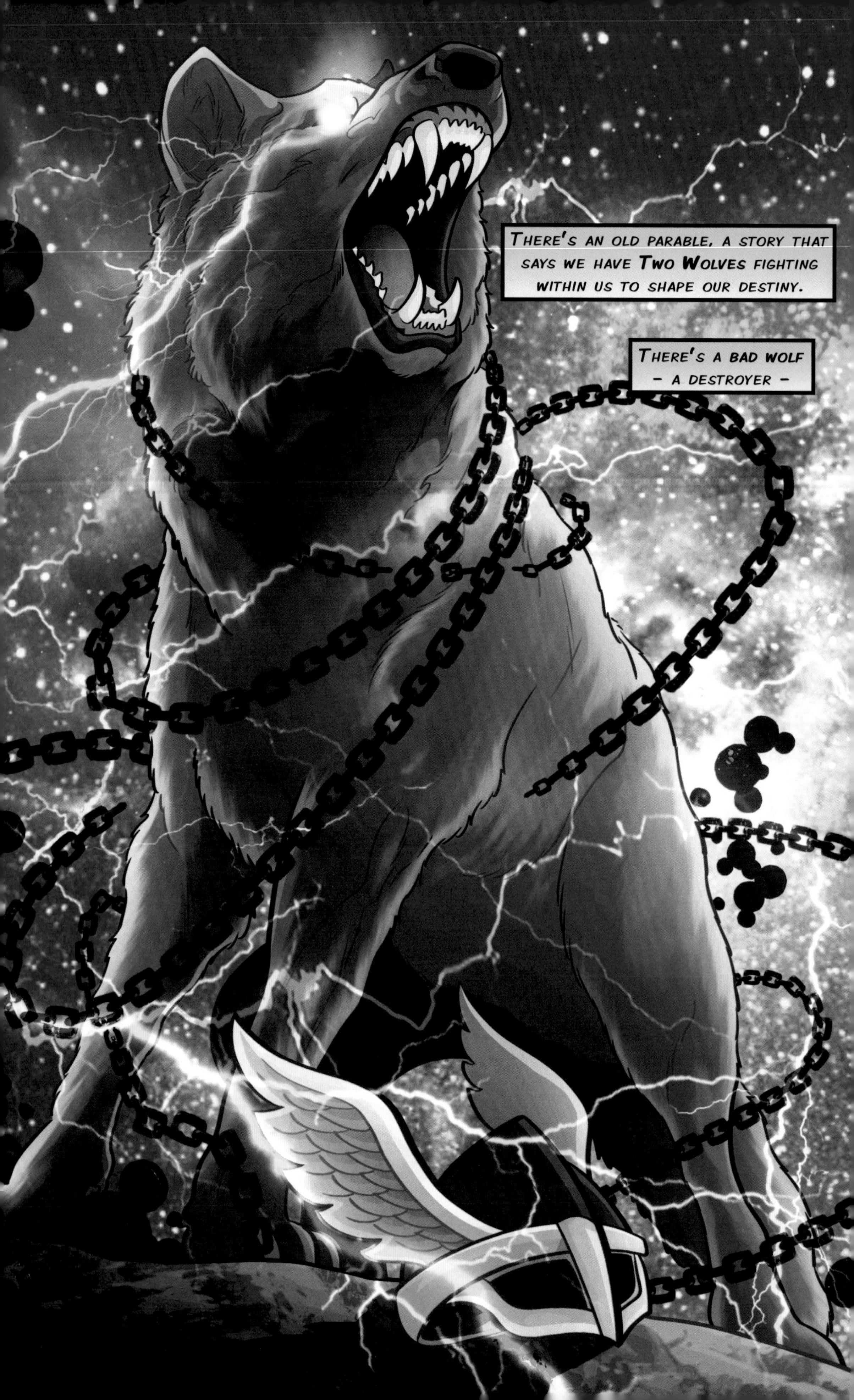
There's an old parable, a story that says we have Two Wolves fighting within us to shape our destiny.
There's a bad wolf - a destroyer -

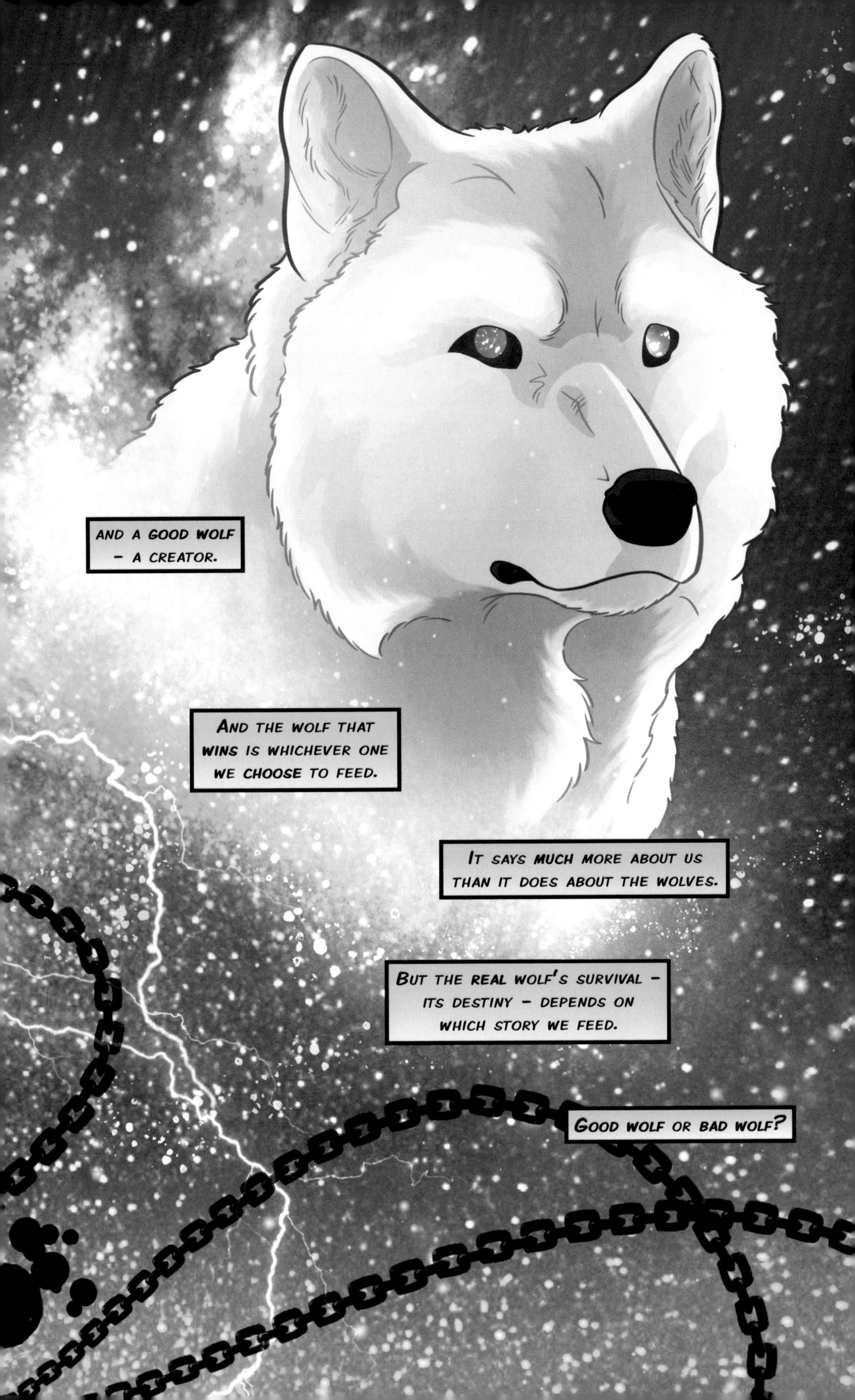

AND A GOOD WOLF – A CREATOR.
AND THE WOLF THAT WINS IS WHICHEVER ONE WE CHOOSE TO FEED.
IT SAYS MUCH MORE ABOUT US THAN IT DOES ABOUT THE WOLVES.
BUT THE REAL WOLF'S SURVIVAL – ITS DESTINY – DEPENDS ON WHICH STORY WE FEED.
GOOD WOLF OR BAD WOLF?

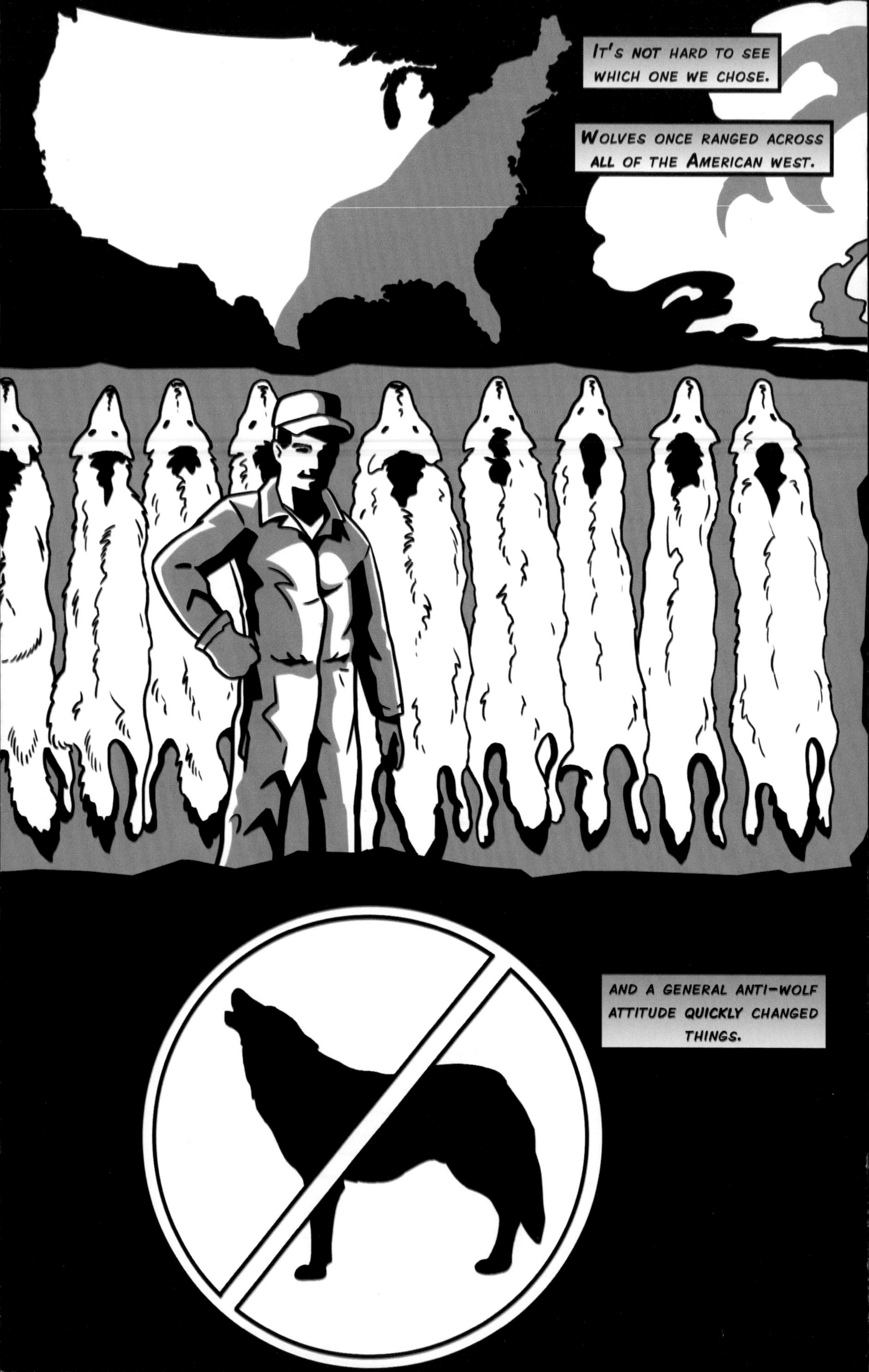
It's not hard to see which one we chose.
Wolves once ranged across all of the American west.
And a general anti-wolf attitude quickly changed things.

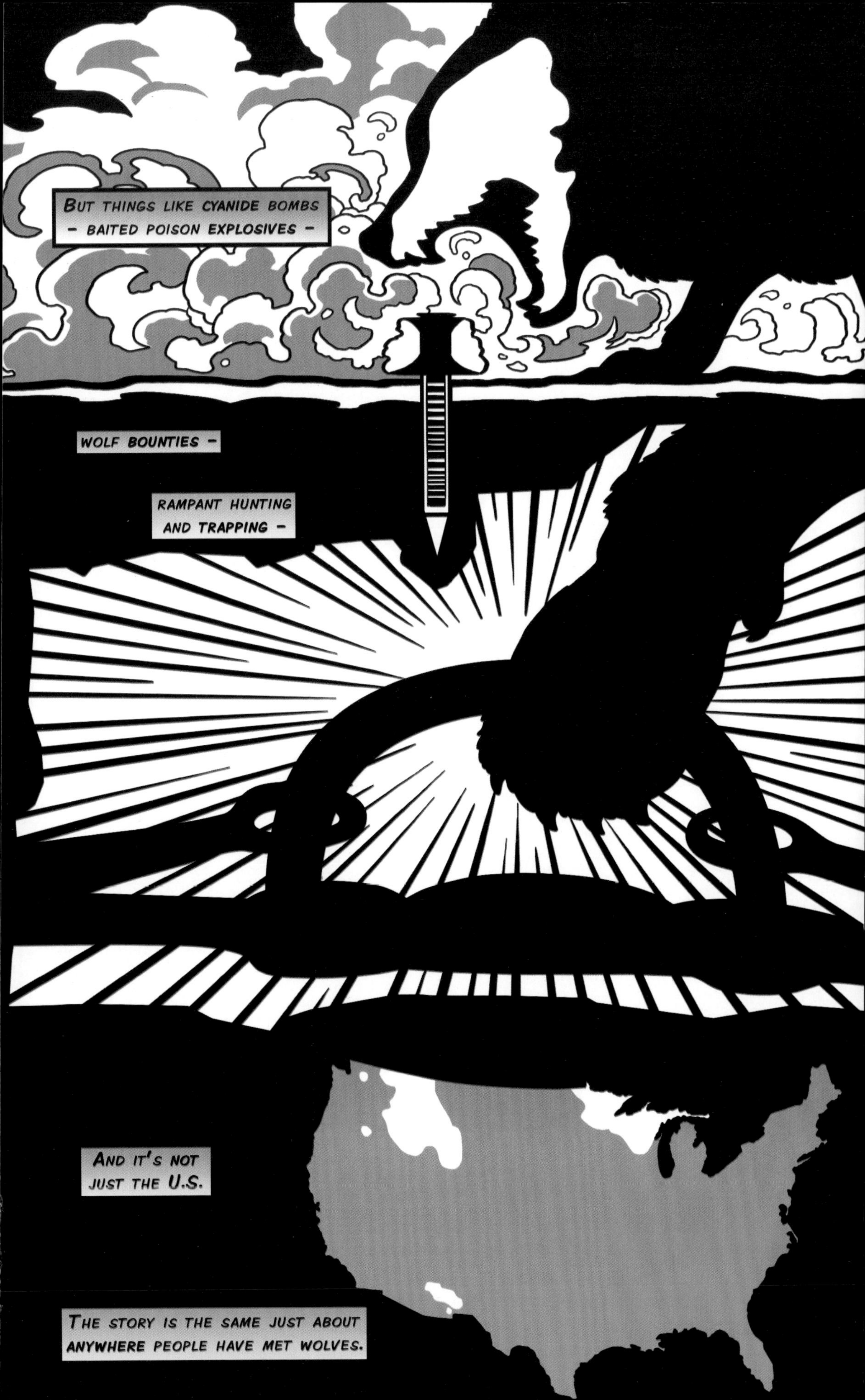
BUT THINGS LIKE CYANIDE BOMBS - BAITED POISON EXPLOSIVES -
WOLF BOUNTIES -
RAMPANT HUNTING AND TRAPPING -
AND IT'S NOT JUST THE U.S.
THE STORY IS THE SAME JUST ABOUT ANYWHERE PEOPLE HAVE MET WOLVES.

RECLAMATION

NORTHERN CALIFORNIA
PRESENT DAY

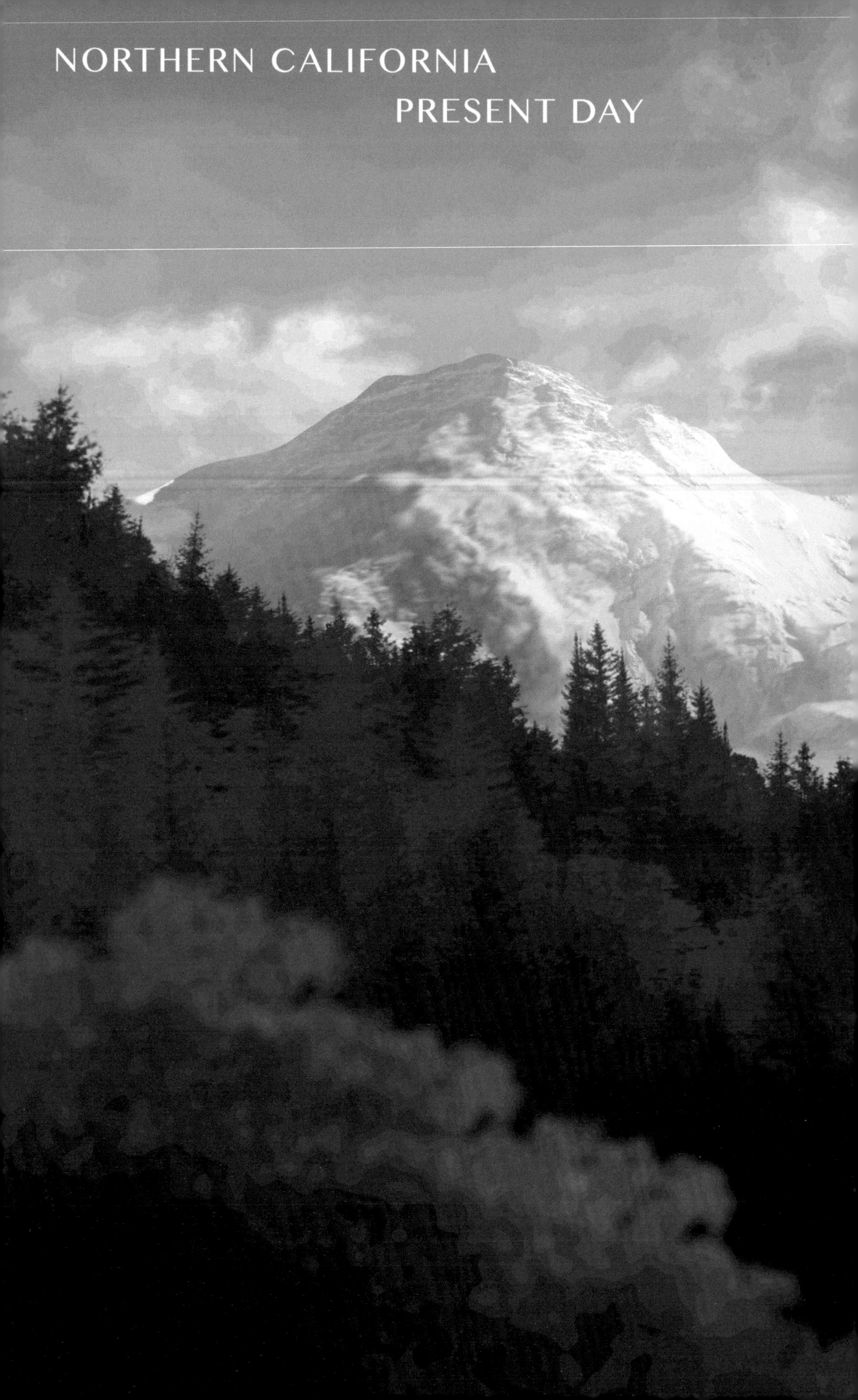

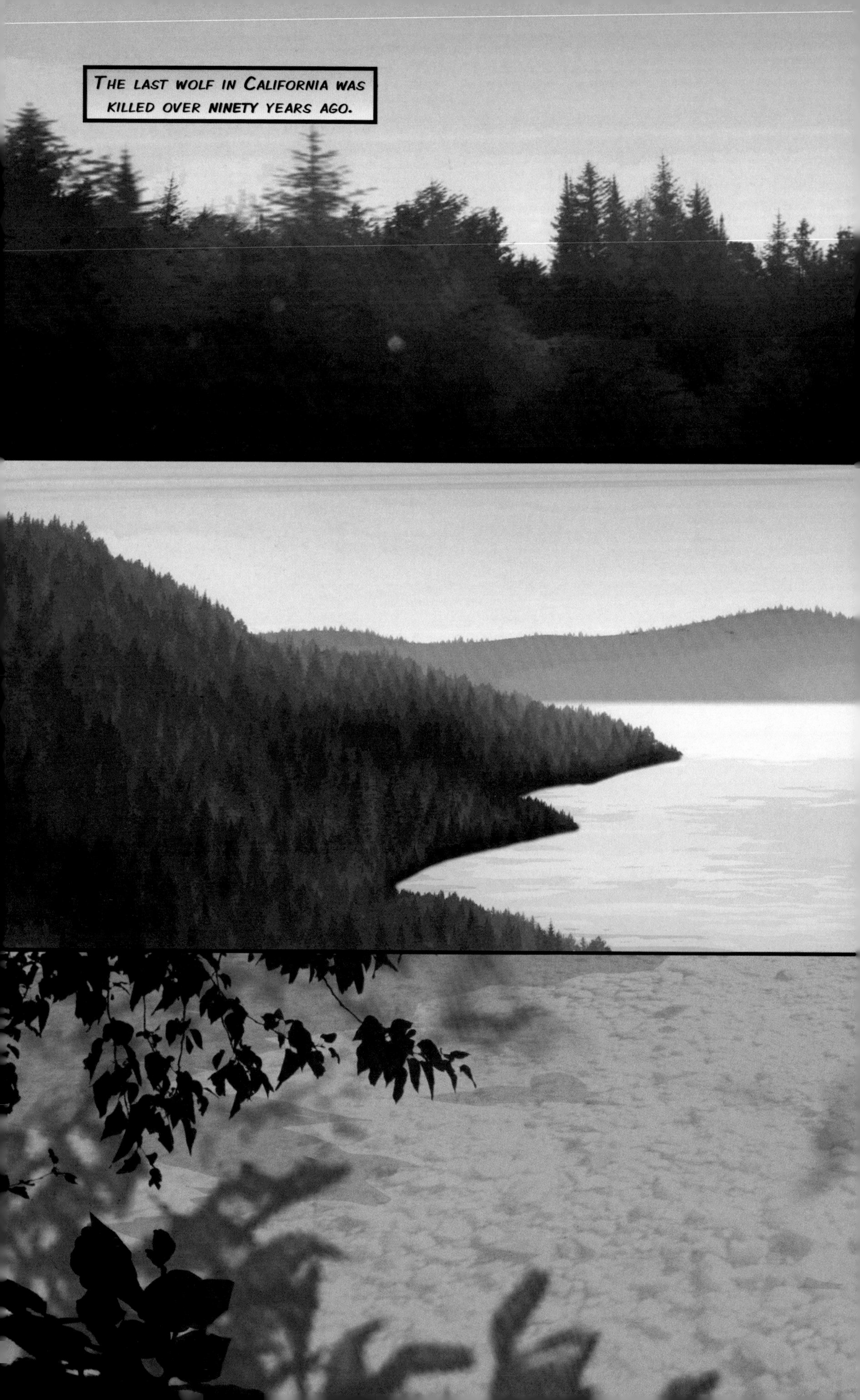
THE LAST WOLF IN CALIFORNIA WAS KILLED OVER NINETY YEARS AGO.

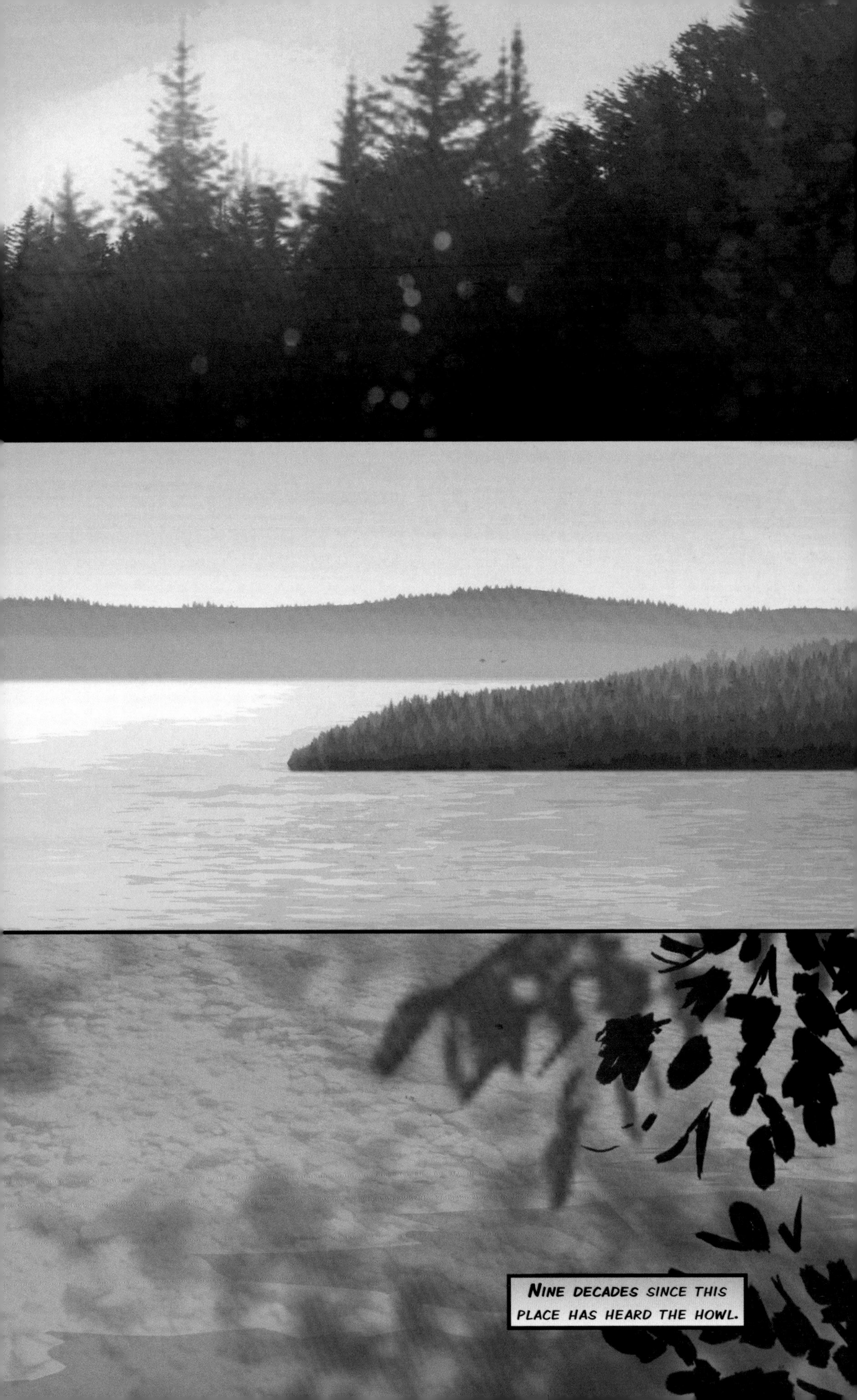
NINE DECADES SINCE THIS PLACE HAS HEARD THE HOWL.

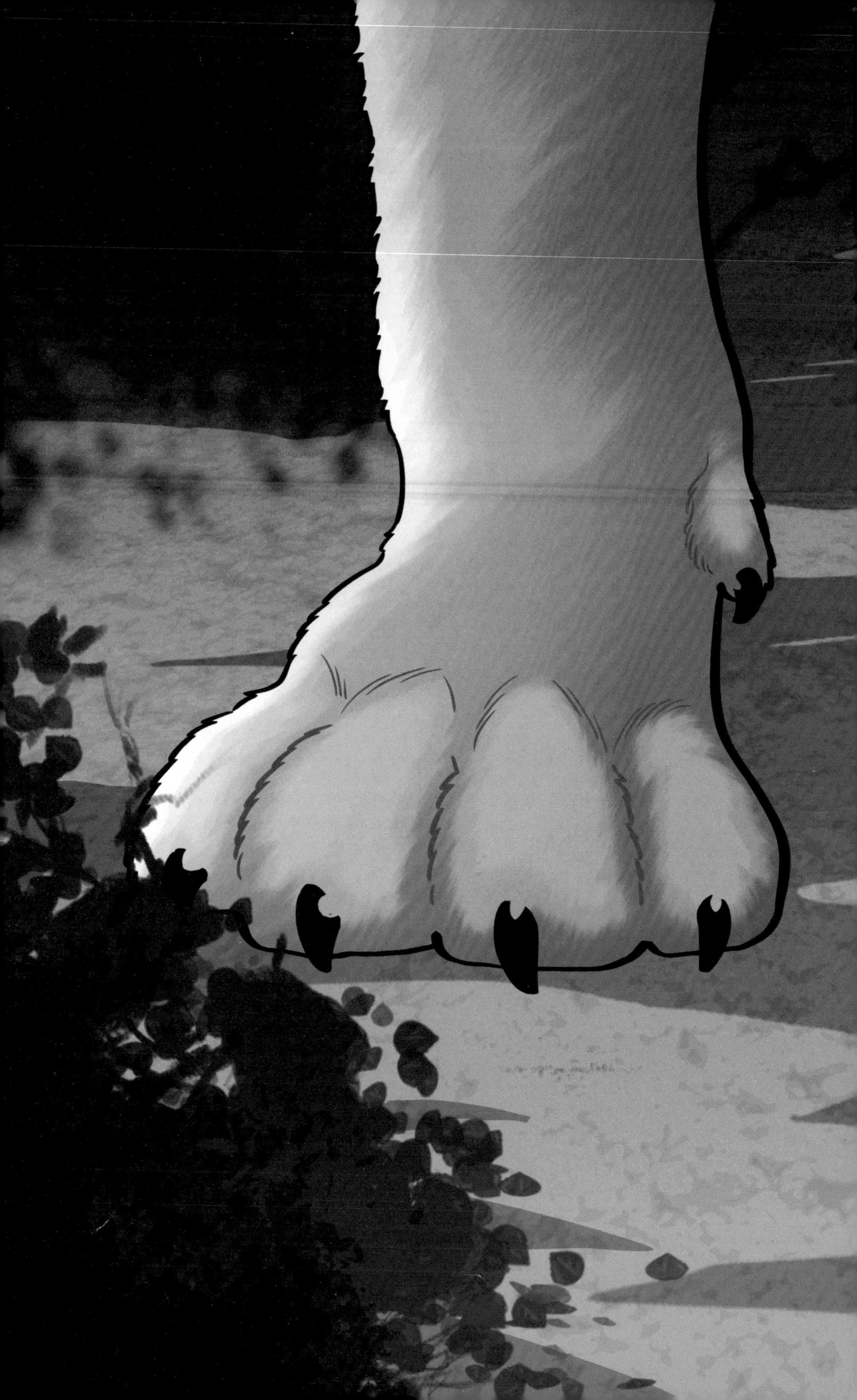

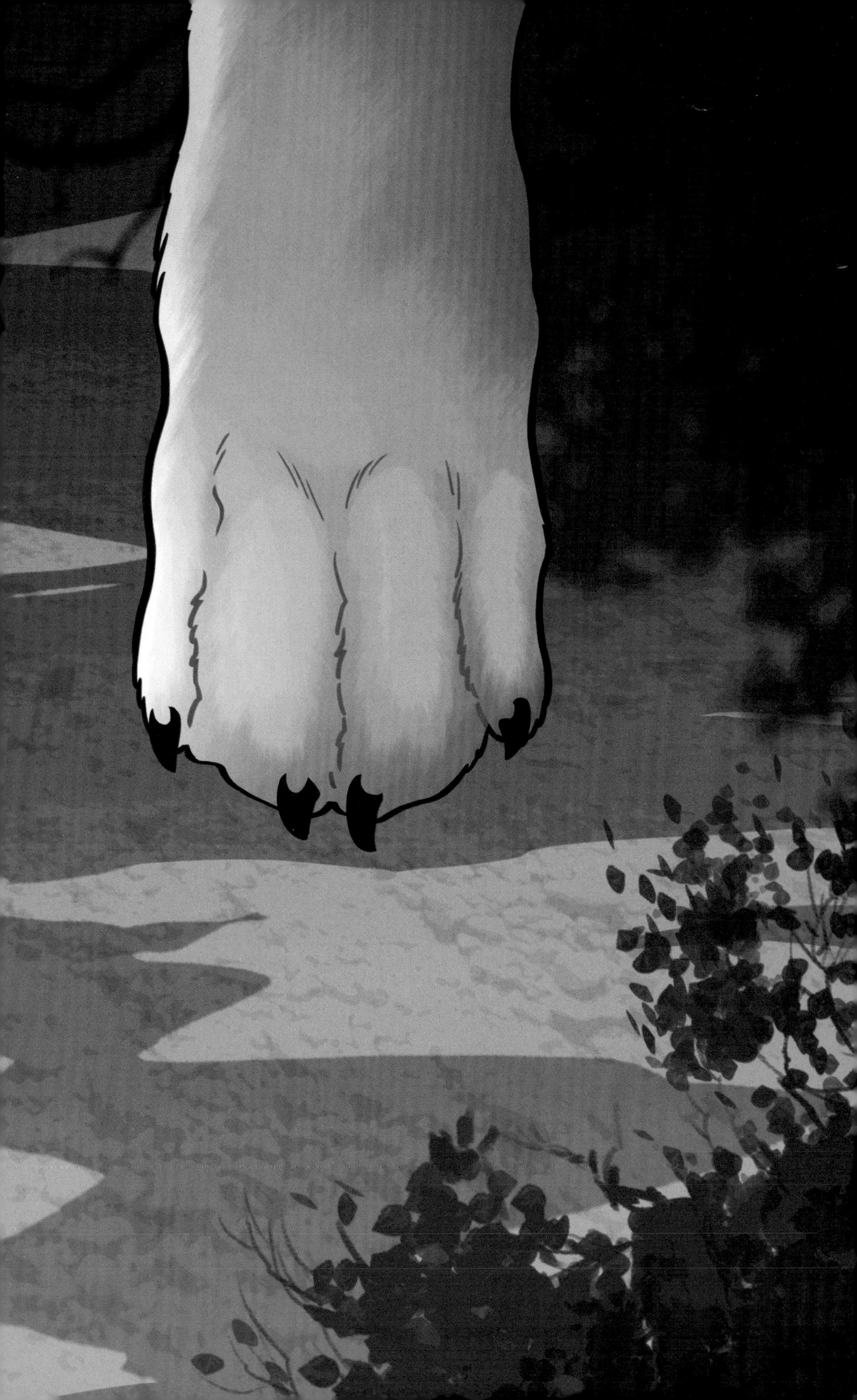

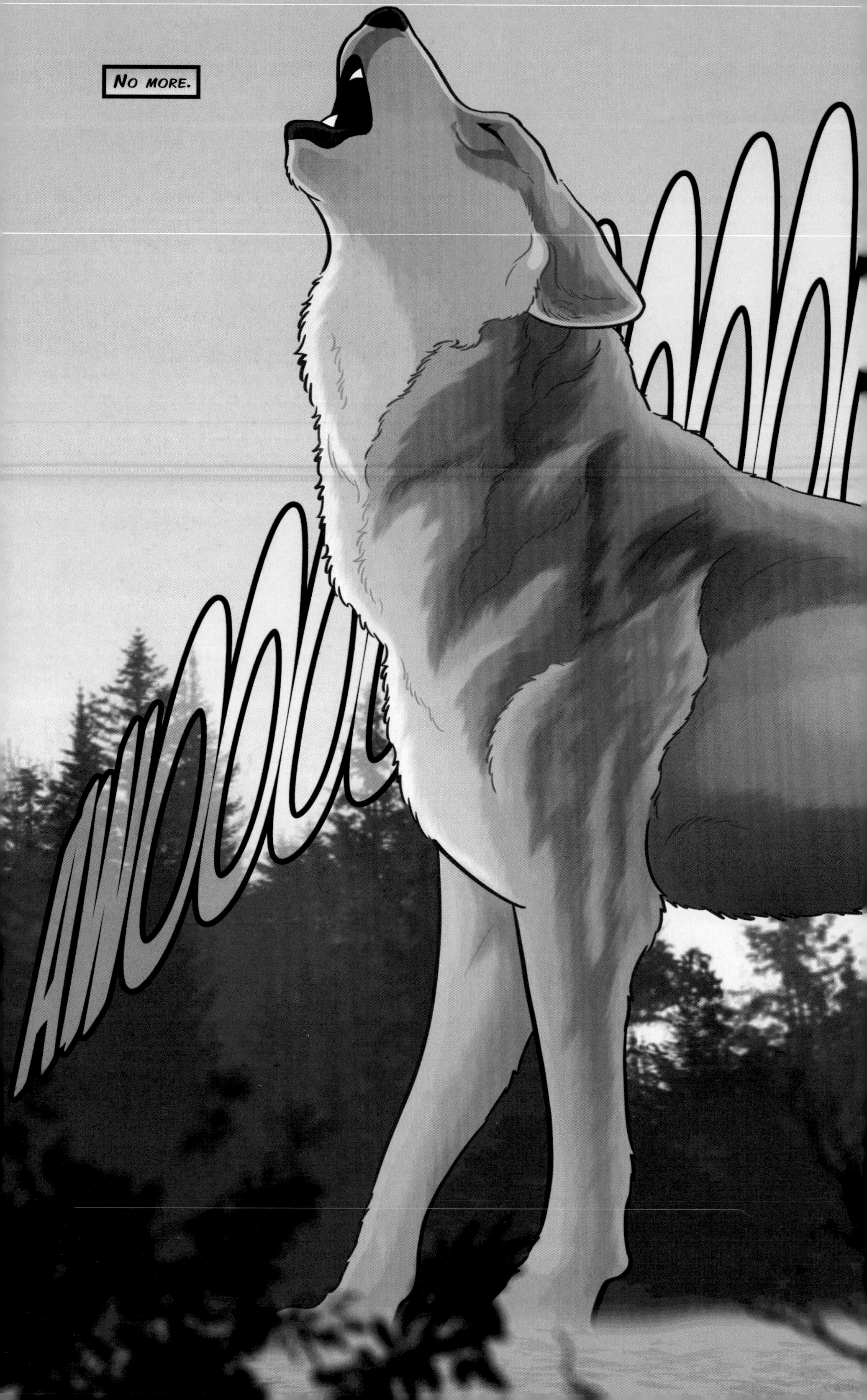
No more.

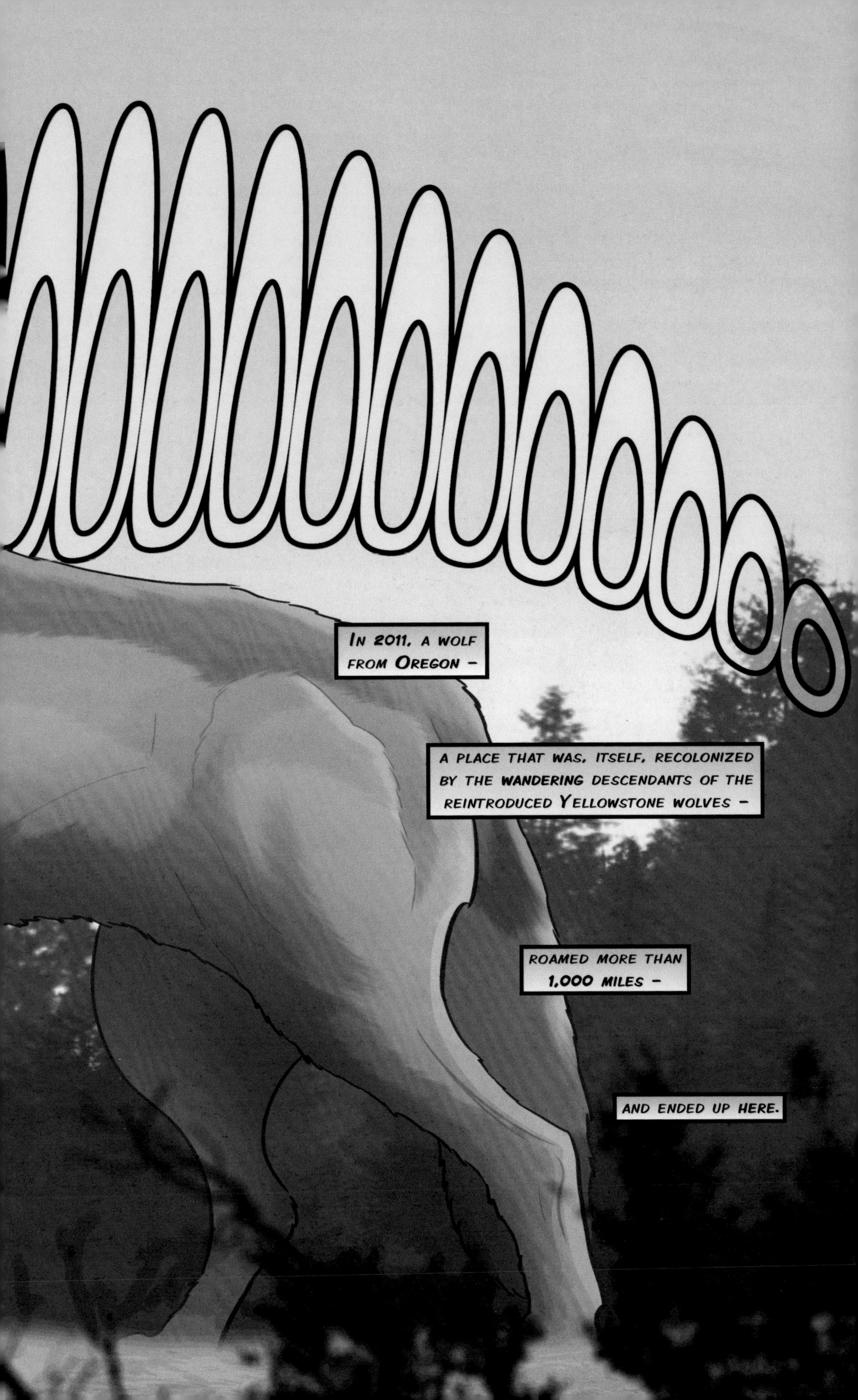
In 2011, a wolf from Oregon –
A place that was, itself, recolonized by the wandering descendants of the reintroduced Yellowstone wolves –
roamed more than 1,000 miles –
and ended up here.

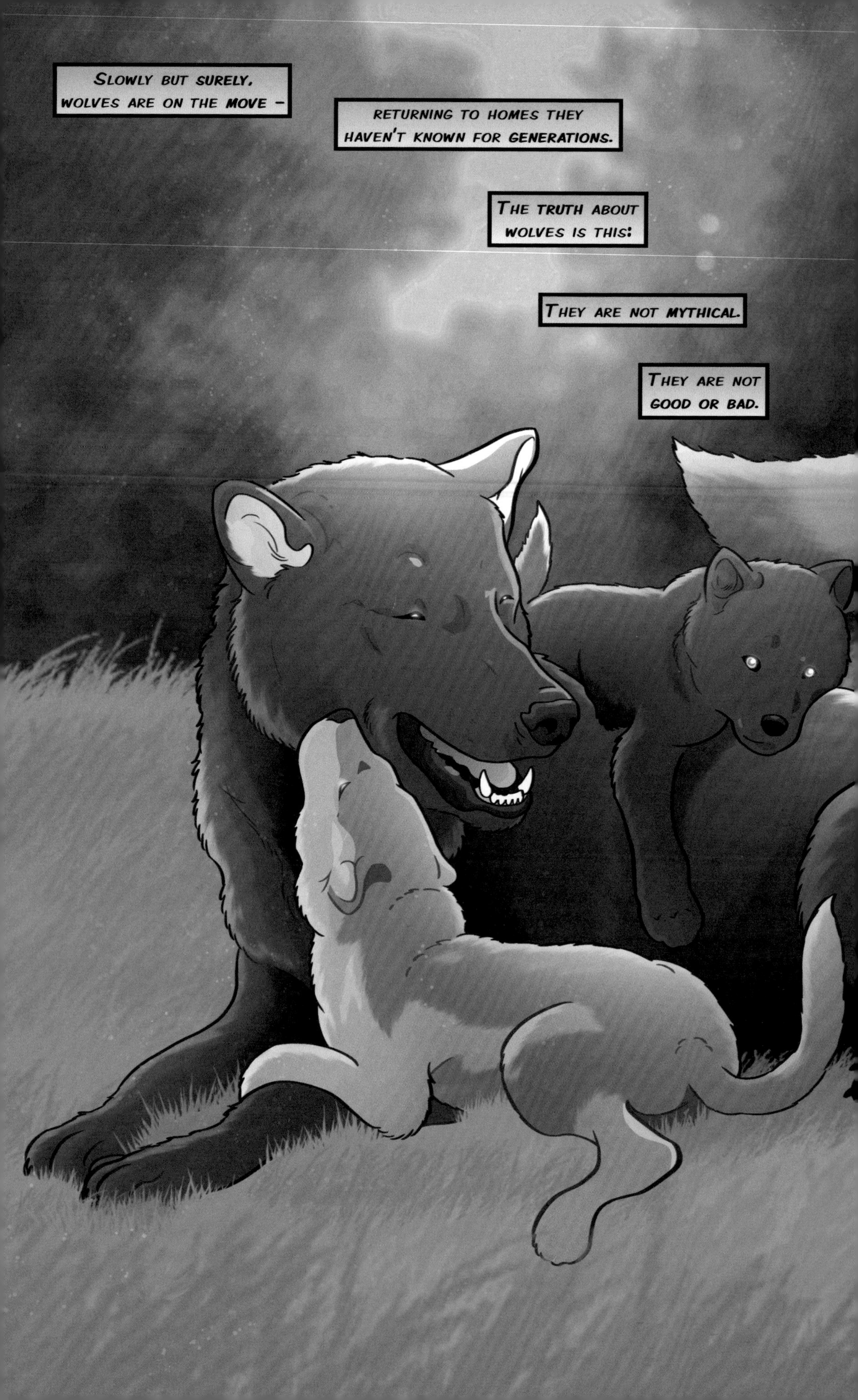
SLOWLY BUT SURELY, WOLVES ARE ON THE MOVE –
RETURNING TO HOMES THEY HAVEN'T KNOWN FOR GENERATIONS.
THE TRUTH ABOUT WOLVES IS THIS:
THEY ARE NOT MYTHICAL.
THEY ARE NOT GOOD OR BAD.

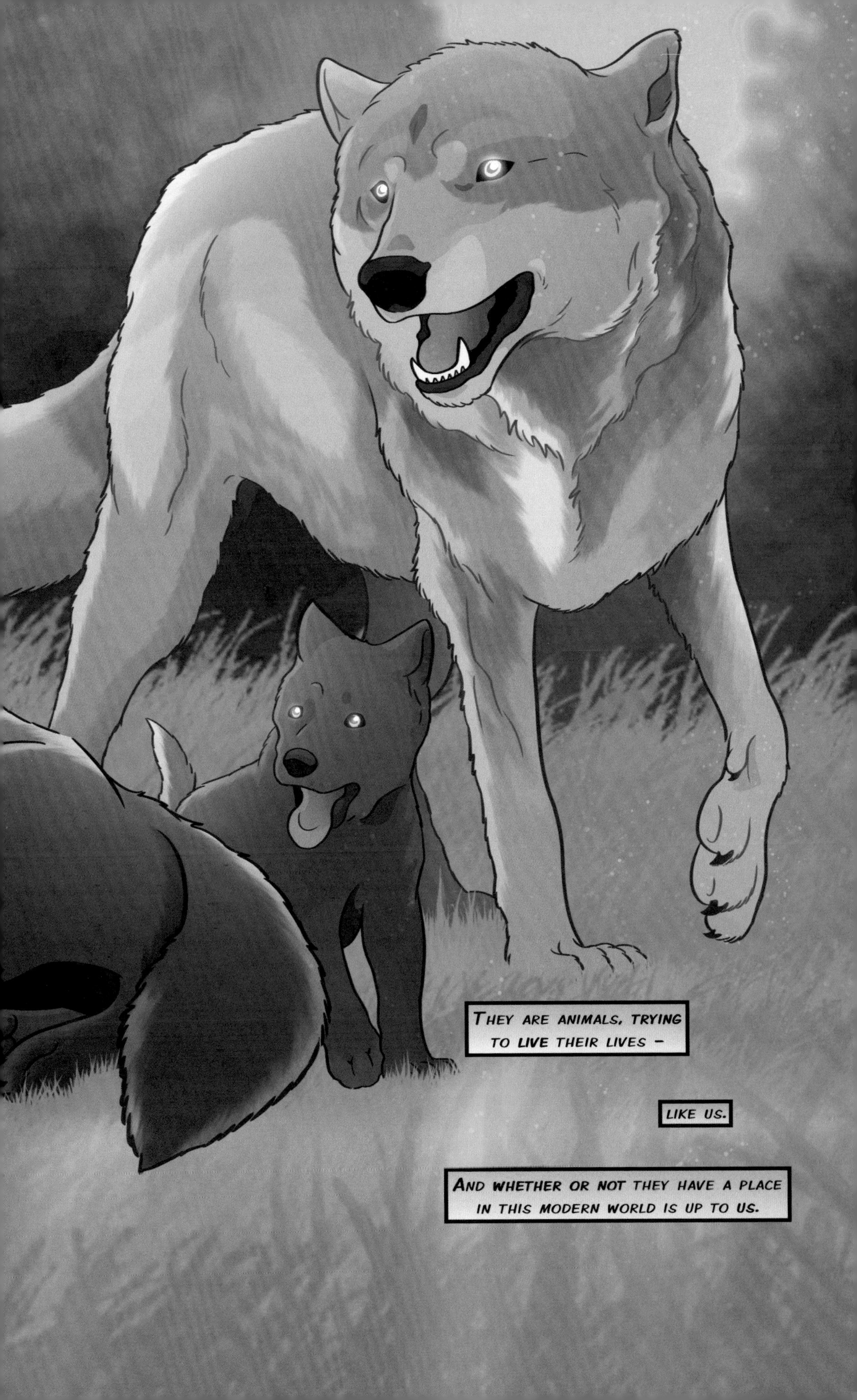
THEY ARE ANIMALS, TRYING TO LIVE THEIR LIVES –
LIKE US.
AND WHETHER OR NOT THEY HAVE A PLACE IN THIS MODERN WORLD IS UP TO US.